A DEGREE IN A BOOK

PSYCHOLOGY

ALAN PORTER

ARCTURUS

ARCTURUS

This edition published in 2019 by Arcturus Publishing Limited
26/27 Bickels Yard, 151–153 Bermondsey Street,
London SE1 3HA

ISBN: 978-1-78828-621-3
AD006054UK

Printed in China

PSYCHOLOGY

CONTENTS

INTRODUCTION

This book provides the reader with an overview of the different areas of psychology that are covered on a typical psychology degree course. What will emerge over the course of these chapters is that psychology is a very varied discipline. Some psychologists are interested in studying processes that are common to all of us, such as learning and memory. Other psychologists study the processes that make us different, in terms of intelligence and personality.

Some psychologists sharply distinguish between normal and abnormal behaviour, while others see these distinctions as lying on a continuum of human behaviour. Some areas of psychology are very technical and require specialist knowledge of statistics or computer programming. Other areas of psychology require the cultivation of listening skills and reflection. What brings together these different areas of psychology is that, despite differences in conceptual vocabulary and differences in research methods, all these different kinds of psychology approach their subject matter systematically and empirically. Psychologists are not content to fall back on speculation. They attempt to support their theories with evidence.

To provide an overview of such a vast field in one short book requires that much material has been left out. Inevitably, this includes information that is interesting and, perhaps, even considered vital by many psychologists. This is inevitable and not necessarily a bad thing. The goal of this book is to provide an overview that might answer some questions but more importantly, stimulate the reader to ask more. And psychology is not a finished science! Psychology is still a relatively young discipline and it is likely that there is more to learn in the future than has been learned in the past.

Each chapter gives a general overview of the topic and introduces important concepts and research methods. In a series of boxes, important studies, individuals or methods are explored in greater depth. This will allow the reader to get a sense of the general 'lie of the land' and also a sense of the style of research carried out in different areas. Wherever possible, diagrams and illustrations have been provided to help the reader make sense of complex ideas.

The chapters can be read in any order and the reader can read each chapter straight through or might consider dipping in and out of the chapter to follow up ideas and people through internet searches as they go along. At the end of the book, there is a section on further reading that provides a short, chapter-by-chapter, bibliography of books suitable for the general reader and textbooks targeted at psychology students. Much literature is available free on the Internet so a list of useful websites has been provided.

Psychology is a challenging, infuriating and rewarding subject. Learning about psychology is a lifelong task. This book can point the reader to some of the areas and topics that might inspire them to consider taking the study of psychology further in the future.

The third International Psychoanalytic Congress was held in Weimar, Germany in 1911. Attended by more than 55 people, it represented the growth of scientific psychology. The subject has grown exponentially since then, but there is still much to learn.

Chapter One

WHAT IS PSYCHOLOGY?

The Scope of Psychology – History of Psychology – Wilhelm Wundt and the Institute for Experimental Psychology

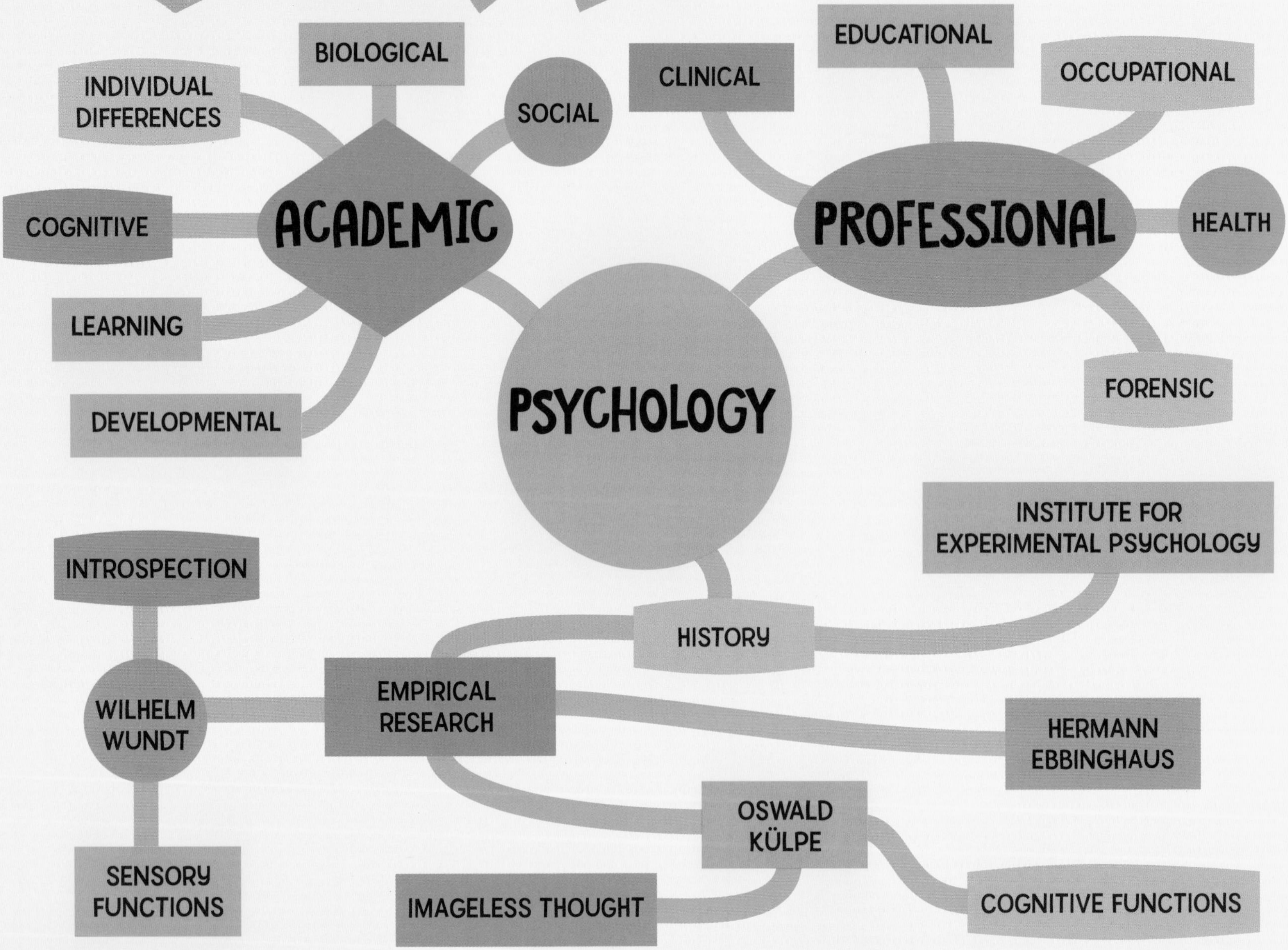

PSYCHOLOGY
ACADEMIC
BIOLOGICAL
INDIVIDUAL DIFFERENCES
SOCIAL
COGNITIVE
LEARNING
DEVELOPMENTAL
PROFESSIONAL
CLINICAL
EDUCATIONAL
OCCUPATIONAL
HEALTH
FORENSIC
HISTORY
INSTITUTE FOR EXPERIMENTAL PSYCHOLOGY
EMPIRICAL RESEARCH
HERMANN EBBINGHAUS
OSWALD KÜLPE
IMAGELESS THOUGHT
COGNITIVE FUNCTIONS
WILHELM WUNDT
INTROSPECTION
SENSORY FUNCTIONS

ACADEMICS AND PROFESSIONALS

Psychology is a body of knowledge, an academic discipline and a profession. As a body of knowledge, psychologists have contributed to our understanding of phenomena as diverse as child development, the treatment of phobias, differences in sociability and how we remember lists of names. As an academic discipline, its place in the university has grown remarkably over the last hundred and thirty or so years. It started with a few specialists trying to study their own experiences systematically. It has now become one of the most popular degree subjects across the world, attracting millions of dollars of funding and educating tens of thousands of students in psychological theory and psychological research methods. With the growth of academic psychology, we have also seen a huge rise in the number of professional psychologists. These draw on psychological research to advise, treat and counsel children and adults in medical settings, schools, work places and private practice.

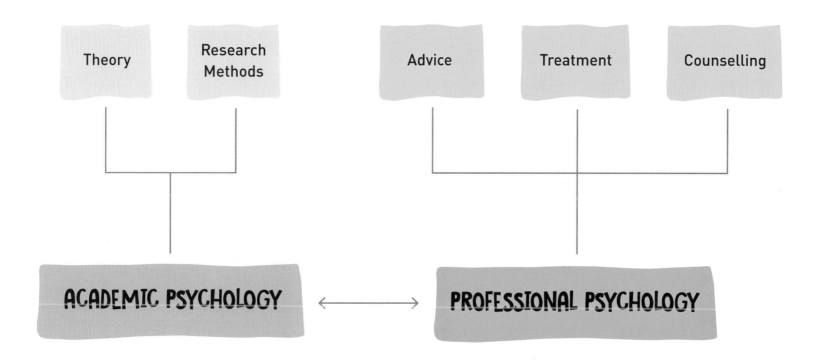

THE SCOPE OF PSYCHOLOGY

It's very difficult to provide a quick summary of psychology or even to give a useful definition of the term 'psychology' itself. This is because there are many different kinds of psychology and these all have different starting points and different methodologies. A typical psychology degree will cover the most important approaches and methods but will still leave out a lot of interesting material. Typically, in a three-year degree, students study social psychology, biological psychology, individual differences (intelligence and personality), cognitive psychology, psychology of learning and developmental psychology. After studying these basic areas, students are then introduced to specialisms that might include clinical psychology, educational psychology, occupational psychology, health psychology and forensic psychology. Completing an undergraduate degree is just the first step to becoming a professional psychologist. For example, to become a clinical or educational psychologist you must complete a three-year professional doctorate before you're qualified to work with patients or pupils. That's after you've completed your degree. This is an important point to bear in mind if you intend to study psychology at university because an undergraduate degree is just the beginning of a long journey to professional qualification.

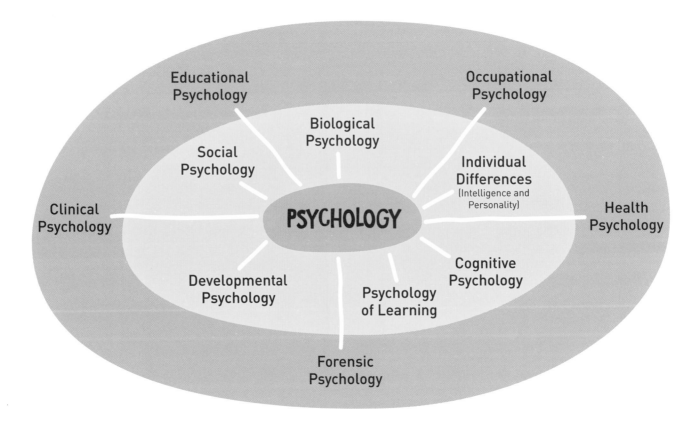

Plan of This Book

Most undergraduate degrees in psychology require students to attend hundreds of hours of lectures and seminars. Students are also required to read, in their own time, many thousands of pages of textbooks, monographs and scientific journal articles (journal articles are how scientists communicate their research findings). It is not possible to summarise all of this material in a short book like this. What is possible is to select some topics from the main areas of psychology in order to illustrate the kind of psychological knowledge you can hope to gain over the course of a degree. 'Suggested reading' sections for each chapter at the end of the book will point you to sources that will help you to extend and deepen your knowledge of psychology.

A BRIEF NOTE ON THE HISTORY OF PSYCHOLOGY

It's worth taking a brief look at the history of contemporary psychology in order to get a sense of the scope of the field. Psychology is still a relatively young science, emerging as an academic discipline in its own right only in the last quarter of the nineteenth century. In 1908, the German experimental psychologist Hermann Ebbinghaus stated, at the beginning of his *Psychology: An Elementary Text-book* (1908), that: *'Psychology has a long past, yet its real history is short'*. This is a phrase that has become important in describing how psychologists understand their discipline. What Ebbinghaus was getting at is that questions about human nature had long been asked by philosophers, theologians and pedagogues (educationalists) and also by physicians, surgeons and biologists. In the course of their work they had often run up against questions about the relationship between mind and body. Psychology's 'long past' comprised, at best, a rich source of anecdotal observations and, at worst, mere armchair speculation with no objective grounding. The 'short history' of psychology began when a generation of thinkers and researchers began to conceive of psychology as a *systematic* and *empirical* science that could produce objective and reliable theories and data. (We look at how Ebbinghaus conducted the first systematic studies of memory in Chapter 3).

Hermann Ebbinghaus was one of the first psychologists to conduct empirical research.

Psychology as science

Willhelm Wundt and the Institute for Experimental Psychology

According to Ebbinghaus, the short history of psychology began when Gustave Fechner (1801–87), Ebbinghaus (1850–1909) himself and, most importantly, Wilhelm Wundt (1832–1920) began to conduct *empirical* research (that is, when they got out of their armchairs and began to collect and analyse data systematically). We will return to the work of Fechner and Ebbinghaus in later chapters.

EMPIRICAL RESEARCH ▶ *the systematic collection and analysis of data.*

Experimental Psychology

NAMES TO KNOW: THE FOUNDERS OF PSYCHOLOGY

Gustave Fechner
(1801–87)

Wilhelm Wundt
(1832–1920)

Hermann Ebbinghaus
(1850–1909)

Oswald Külpe
(1862–1915)

One of Wundt's key contributions was to set up the first Institute for Experimental Psychology at the University of Leipzig in 1879 and to oversee the supervision of a whole generation of PhD students from around the world. These students went back to their homelands and founded their own laboratories of experimental psychology in the USA, UK, France and Italy.

Wilhelm Wundt set up the Institute for Experimental Psychology at the University of Leipzig in 1879.

Psychology as the study of conscious experience

The subject matter of Wundt's psychology was conscious experience. He realised that studying conscious experience was problematic because it required a conscious observer to become conscious of their own observing, leading to dizzying complexities. For example, in the case of self-observation (*introspection*), does the very fact that the observer is observing his or herself change what he or she is observing?

Wundt's way of approaching the problem of self-observation was to develop a systematic and controlled method of *introspection* that, he argued, was as objective as the methods of chemists and physicists. Wundt believed that the methods of introspection that made up a lot of the accounts of human nature were flawed because they relied on memory and the particular choices of phenomena on which to introspect. This might be introspecting on the experience of something rather general and abstract, like happiness, or something very specific, like the experience of hearing a pin drop.

> **INTROSPECTIVE PSYCHOLOGY** ▶ *the study of simple sensory processes.*

Wundt limited introspective psychology to the study of *simple sensory processes* such as auditory tones and insisted that introspection was carried out in the present. The participants in these experiments, usually Wundt himself or his PhD students, were highly trained so that they could concentrate intensely on the stimuli that were presented to them. These stimuli (they might be auditory tones or coloured patches) were carefully measured and were repeated with variations again and again to ensure the results were reliable.

Introspection

Simple sensory processes

The precision of the Hipp Chronoscope allowed early psychologists such as Wundt to measure reaction times with great accuracy.

WUNDT'S ACCOUNT OF HOW WE MAKE SENSE OF THE WORLD

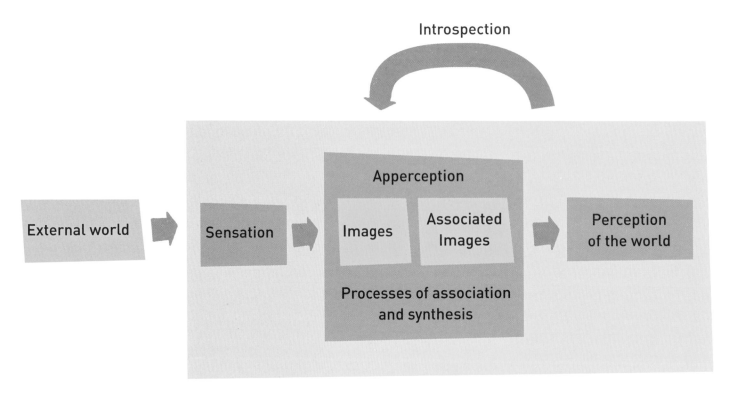

Despite Wundt's best intentions to make his science of consciousness reliable and systematic, controversy followed almost as soon as he had set up his laboratory and started publishing his results. Despite his warnings, his followers and other psychologists who took up his methods extended the scope of the new psychology to include not just simple sensory stimuli but also higher ***cognitive functions,*** such as problem solving. For example, Oswald Külpe (1862–1915) asked his experimental participants at the University of Würzburg to introspect on their experience of being asked the question in the context of a laboratory session 'Where are we going afterwards?' One participant reported that after being asked the question the following passed through his mind: 'Acoustic-motor pronunciation of the words "To the cafe". But the words "Wherever you want" competed. State of consciousness which can be called doubt.'

Even more problematic than applying introspection to what, for Wundt, was inappropriate

Cognitive functions

phenomena was his contention that all mental (psychological) phenomena must be made up of conscious sensory images. These are images derived from any of our senses: sight, hearing, taste, smell, touch, relative sense of the parts of our body and so on. In Wurzburg, Külpe and his followers declared that they had come across examples where, under carefully controlled conditions, participants had thoughts with no trace of images, with thoughts simply appearing spontaneously in the stream of consciousness. They referred to this kind of phenomena as imageless thought.

At the University of Würzburg, Oswald Külpe began to explore higher cognitive functions.

The New Psychology Fragments

The whole point of Wundt's methodology was that it would end arguments based on armchair speculation or naïve introspection once and for all because psychology was now grounded in objective methods. The controversy about the existence of imageless thoughts brought the objectivity of the new *Controversy* psychology into question. There was no conclusive way it could be settled because the controversy at bottom concerned a question of subjective experience leading to a kind of introspective 'he said she said'. This did not stop psychology growing but it did stop psychology developing as a unified academic discipline. Wundt at Leipzig and Külpe at Würzburg agreed to disagree, and their students went their own ways.

EXPERIMENTAL PSYCHOLOGY ▶ *study of conscious experience by trained observers.*

Wundt had limited his experimental psychology to the study of conscious experience by trained observers. What about the experiences of children or untrained observers? What about the study of the mentally ill? Wundt had provided a rationale for the development of psychology independent of philosophy and physiology but had given it a very narrow scope. Those who came after Wundt widened the scope of psychology and took the discipline in different directions. They honoured Wundt's insistence that psychology was a systematic and empirical science but they abandoned his definition of psychology as the study of conscious experience. Over the following century, they were to take psychology in many different directions. The following chapters will map out where these different directions have brought us so far.

WHAT IS PSYCHOLOGY?

Psychology's long history began with the questioning of the ancient Greek philosophers. They asked what it is to be human and sought to understand the nature of knowledge. For Plato (*c*.424–*c*.347BC), the human mind could glimpse the eternal beyond the earthly. He believed that the body was the tomb of the soul and introduced a dualism into how we think about the relationship between soul and body. Aristotle (384–322BC), in contrast, looked to the natural world and examined how our human capacities for thought and reason fitted into a hierarchy of being from the plants to the gods.

This ordered view of nature and our place in it lasted for hundreds of years. René Descartes (1596–1650) challenged this view and argued for a new set of dualisms: mind and matter, and mind and body. The implication of his rationalistic philosophy was that knowledge was innate and the body, including the brain, were mechanisms more complex but no different in kind from clockwork toys.

The British empiricists, John Locke (1632–1704), David Hume (1711–76) and George Berkeley (1685–1753), rejected Descartes' view ('Cartesianism') and argued that the mind was a blank slate and our knowledge of the world was the result of the association of ideas. Immanuel Kant (1724–1804) attempted to bridge rationalism and empiricism and put in place a model of the mind composed of faculties that integrated sensory information with abstract categories or reason.

In the nineteenth century, physiologists began to investigate how this might be possible from a biological point of view. Hermann von Helmholtz (1821–94) investigated vision and nerve physiology, measuring the speed of nerve conduction in 1852. Helmholtz's assistant, Wilhelm Wundt (1832–1920), proposed that these neurophysiological methods could be adapted to study consciousness. He opened his Institute of Experimental Psychology in Leipzig in 1879, which played a key role in the development of the modern science of psychology.

Descartes established the idea of a division between mind and matter.

Psychic Salivation and Animal Behaviour – The Conditional Reflex – John Watson and the Behaviourist Manifesto – Burrhus Frederic Skinner and the Puzzle Box – Operant Conditioning – Gestalt Psychology – Wolfgang Köhler and the Anthropoid Research Station

REINFORCEMENT

WOLFGANG KÖHLER

EDWARD THORNDIKE

B.F. SKINNER

OPERANT CONDITIONING

GESTALT

PUZZLE BOXES

LEARNING

PSYCHIC SALIVATION

REFLEXOLOGY

BEHAVIOURISM

COMPARATIVE PSYCHOLOGY

PAVLOV'S DOGS

JOHN BROADUS WATSON

CONDITIONED

UNCONDITIONED

NATURE V. NURTURE

LITTLE ALBERT

STIMULUS AND RESPONSE

A NEW APPROACH

As we saw in the previous chapter, arguments about the reliability and objectivity of *introspection* began to plague the new discipline of psychology. One way to deal with these problems was simply to banish the subjective and experiential from scientific psychology once and for all. In this way, researchers get rid of the whole mental vocabulary around thinking, feeling and acting, or show how these concepts could be described in terms that were directly observable and measurable. By abandoning Wundt's scientific introspection, the scientific approach to psychology would be reinvigorated. This is exactly what the advocates of so-called *Behaviourism* proposed. In this chapter, we will examine how the Behaviourists set about making learning the central focus of psychology. We will also introduce some alternative ways of thinking about learning.

NAMES TO KNOW: BEHAVIOURISM

Ivan Pavlov *(1849–1936)*
– Reflexology

John Broadus Watson
(1878–1958) – Behaviourist Manifesto

BEHAVIOURISM ▶ *explaining the mind through public behaviour.*

Ivan Pavlov was a Nobel Prize-winning physiologist and his study of dogs' reflexes revolutionised psychology.

Pavlov's dogs salivated whenever food was placed in their mouth.

PSYCHIC SALIVATION AND ANIMAL BEHAVIOUR

The roots of *behaviourism* lie in the *reflexology* of the Russian physiologist Ivan Pavlov (1849–1936) and the American *comparative psychologist* John Broadus Watson (1878–1958). Pavlov was a gifted surgeon and Nobel Prize-winning physiologist who had demonstrated that the mammalian digestive system was not organized like a long string of beads on a necklace, with each bead a separate element, as had previously been thought. It was, in reality, a highly-integrated system with lots of interconnections that was co-ordinated by the central nervous system. Experimenting on dogs, Pavlov surgically inserted small tubes through their cheeks and into their stomachs to collect their digestive juices. He knew that the dogs salivated automatically if a piece of food was placed in their mouth (see Chapter 4 for a more detailed description of the nervous system and reflexes). His next step was to determine whether anything else, not directly connected with the appearance of food, might trigger the same response.

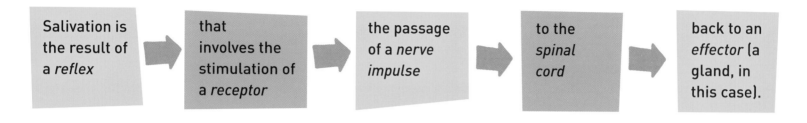

Salivation is the result of a *reflex* → that involves the stimulation of a *receptor* → the passage of a *nerve impulse* → to the *spinal cord* → back to an *effector* (a gland, in this case).

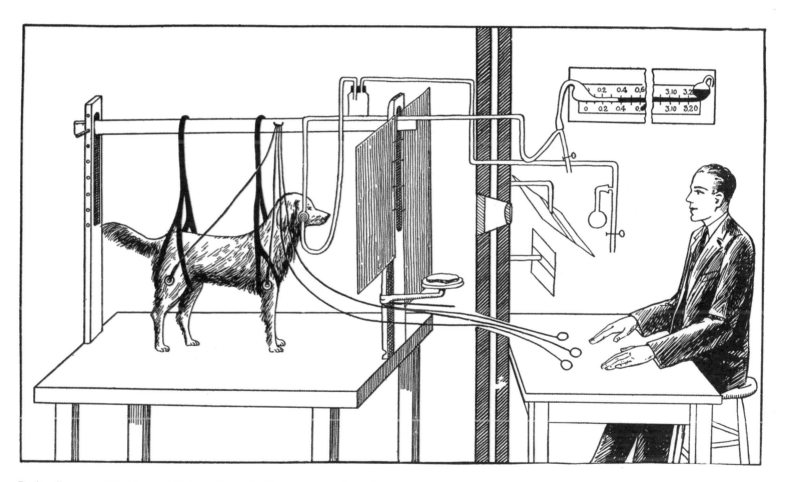

Pavlov discovered that he could trigger the salivation response through something entirely unconnected with food, simply by a process of association.

Pavlov had observed that the rattle of keys, as his staff opened up the laboratory on a morning ready to bring the dogs their breakfast, was enough to make the dogs slobber and salivate without even seeing or smelling any food. He was also aware from personal experience that if we are hungry our mouths sometimes start watering at the sight of an appetising meal or if we see a slice of juicy lemon. Even the verbal description of a juicy lemon might make our mouths water. Is your mouth watering now?

Psychic salivation

Pavlov called this phenomenon **psychic salivation** because it was brought about by a *mental connection* rather than a physical connection and was intrigued by the way a reflex action could be triggered by something to which it had no natural connection and was clearly the result of previous experience, ordered through a process of **association** – as, in this case, the rattle of keys with the presentation of food. After all, there were no bunches of keys to rattle when wild dogs were evolving from packs of wolves or, for that matter, pictures of lemons when humans were evolving on the plains of Africa. As a consequence, Pavlov moved the focus of his research away from pure physiology to the study of reflexes and their modification through learning.

Association

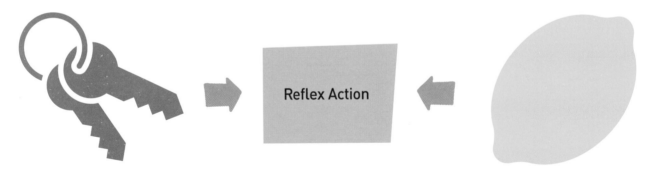

A reflex could be brought about by something entirely unconnected.

THE CONDITIONAL REFLEX

The basic terminology that Pavlov introduced to help him understand the development of psychic salivation starts with the distinction between **unconditioned** and **conditioned** reflexes.

Unconditioned and conditioned reflexes

'Unconditioned' means automatic; 'conditioned' means learned. The unconditioned reflex is triggered by an unconditioned stimulus and results in an unconditioned response. Human unconditioned reflexes include the eye blink that automatically occurs if someone blows in your eye, or the patella reflex that occurs when we receive a sharp blow just below the kneecap and the leg straightens. The conditioned reflex is the result of training in which an unconditioned stimulus is paired with a stimulus that would not otherwise lead to an unconditioned response. For example, rattling keys would not normally cause dogs to salivate. It only occurs when dogs learn that the rattling of keys is always followed by the presentation of food.

	UNCONDITIONED	CONDITIONED
Nature	Automatic	Learned
Reflex	Stimulus and response	Result of training
Example	An eye blink	A dog salivating at the sound of a bell

This pairing of unconditioned and conditioned stimulus is at the heart of what has become known under a number of different names: **Pavlovian**, **Classical** or **Respondent Conditioning**.

PAVLOVIAN CONDITIONING ▶ *the pairing of the unconditioned and conditioned stimulus.*

Using the apparatus shown previously, Pavlov showed that any given phenomenon can be made a temporary signal of the object that stimulates the salivary glands. A dog can be trained to salivate at the sound of a bell or a buzzer or by switching a light on or off.

Stimulus Pairing

The basic form of Pavlovian Conditioning comprises the simultaneous pairing of an *unconditional stimulus* (US) with a *conditioning stimulus* (CS or 'arbitrary stimulus') on successive occasions or trials in a training phase. After repeated pairings, during which the US reinforces the *conditional* or *conditioned response* (CR), the presentation of the US on its own is sufficient to produce a CR. For Pavlov, reinforcement required that US and CS be *contiguous* – that is, one immediately following the other – and *continuous*, or unbroken. If other stimuli occur between pairings of US and CS, or without further pairings, the CS eventually no longer elicits the CR. Conditioning is then said to be *extinguished*.

CLASSICAL CONDITIONING PROCEDURE

Before conditioning

CS (tone) ➡ Does not have capability to produce CR (conditioned response)

US (food) ➡ UR (unconditioned response – salivation)

During conditioning

CS (tone) ➡

US (food) ➡ UR (salivation)

After conditioning

CS (tone) ➡ CR (salivation)

During the early years of the twentieth century, Pavlov's work began to be translated into English and German and came to the attention of psychologists.

NAMES TO KNOW: BEHAVIOURISM

Edward Thorndike
(1874–1949)

Burrhus Frederic Skinner
(1904–90)

JOHN WATSON AND THE BEHAVIOURIST MANIFESTO

Origins of behaviourism

John Broadus Watson (1878–1958) began his academic career studying animal behaviour. He submitted a PhD thesis in 1903 on the 'psychic education' of the white rat. He took up a professorship at Johns Hopkins University in Baltimore, USA, conducting more animal research – this time on the behaviour of two species of seabird, noddy and sooty turns. Impatient with the apparent lack of progress in psychology and with his expertise in animal behaviour, Pavlov's discovery of the principles of conditioning convinced Watson that the tools were at hand to revolutionise psychology. In 1913, in a lecture at Columbia University entitled 'Psychology as the Behaviorist Views It', Watson trumpeted a new approach to psychology that was a *'purely objective, experimental branch of natural science'* and offered the opportunity to control behaviour and regulate our own evolution.

Little Albert and Conditioned Emotional Reactions

To test his new approach to psychology, Watson set in motion one of the most famous – and infamous – experiments in the history of psychology. He sought to establish whether an infant could be conditioned to fear an animal (a conditioned emotional response) and whether that fear would transfer to other animals or to inanimate objects.

Albert B

Watson and his research assistant Rosalind Rayner first exposed a nine-month-old child 'Albert B' to animals including a rabbit, monkey, rat and a dog. Albert showed no fear of these animals. However, he did show fear when, unexpectedly, an iron bar was struck with a hammer behind his back. This action produced crying (an emotional response) and an attempt to move away (avoidance behaviour). Two months later, Watson and Rayner began the training phase of their experiment. The following timetable outlines their procedures and the responses of 'Albert B'.

John Broadus Watson was responsible for one of the most controversial experiments in the history of psychology in the 'Little Albert' study.

Albert exposed to rat, rabbit monkey, dog. No fear.

11 months 3 days Rat presented and iron bar struck with hammer (twice).

11 months 15 days Rat presented followed by wooden blocks, dog, etc.

1 year 21 days *Albert showed fear when touching the Santa Claus mask, the sealskin coat, the rat, the rabbit, and the dog. At the same time, however, he initiated contact with the coat and the rabbit, showing "strife between withdrawal and the tendency to manipulate".*

8 months 26 days Iron bar struck by hammer (repeated 3 times). Crying and attempt to move away (avoidance behaviour).

11 months 10 days Rat presented and iron bar struck with hammer (5 times).

11 months 20 days Rat presented and iron bar struck with hammer. Rabbit presented and iron bar struck with hammer. Dog presented and iron bar struck with hammer.

Nature or Nurture?
Watson was one of the strongest proponents of the importance of nurture in human development. In his book *Behaviorism* (1924) he wrote:

'Give me a dozen healthy infants ... and my own specified world to bring them up in and I'll guarantee to take any one at random and train him to become any type of specialist I might select—doctor, lawyer, artist, merchant-chief and, yes, even beggar-man and thief, regardless of his talents, penchants, tendencies, abilities, vocations, and race of his ancestors' (Watson, 1924, p. 104).

The 'Little Albert' study has become one of the most cited experiments in the history of psychology. The ethical rules that psychologists must follow today would now prohibit a child being treated as Albert was. Despite attempts to track Albert down in later life, he was never found and so we do not know what, if any, long-term trauma he may have suffered. What Watson and Rayner's experiment did show was that emotional responses could be learned and that the principles of Pavlovian Conditioning could be demonstrated on humans as well as animals.

At the end of the 1920s, Watson disappeared from academic psychology when his wife sued him for divorce and an affair with his research assistant Rosalind Rayner then became public. Behaviourism did not die but Pavlovian Conditioning as a paradigm for all learning was challenged and superseded by a new set of learning principles set out by B.F. Skinner under the title of Operant Conditioning.

BURRHUS FREDERIC SKINNER (1904–90) AND THE PUZZLE BOX

B. F. Skinner developed a sophisticated puzzle box that could require a combination of responses to trigger a reward.

Puzzle boxes

Fred Skinner (he apparently preferred this less formal form of address) studied psychology at Harvard, eventually becoming a professor there in 1948. Skinner was greatly influenced by Watson, Pavlov (he always kept an autographed photo of Pavlov in his office throughout his long career) and Thorndike (see box below). He was interested to find out what happened when an animal was presented with a stimulus like Pavlov's dogs – exposed to bells and tones and food by the experimenter – but unable to interact with the environment directly. Unlike the cats in Thorndike's Puzzle boxes, which allowed only one response for the cat to get to the food, Skinner developed his own much more sophisticated puzzle box. These allowed multiple responses and the setting up of combinations of responses to produce a reward. The new kind of puzzle box became known as a 'Skinner Box' after its inventor.

Thorndike and the Puzzle Box

Edward Thorndike (1874–1949) studied animal learning independently of Pavlov. He placed hungry cats in a so-called 'puzzle box' and timed how long it would take them to escape the box to reach some tasty cat food placed near the entrance. The cat could open the door if it touched a piece of wood or treadle that was connected by a length of string to the door catch. Thorndike found that, over repeated trials, it took less and less time for the cat to touch the piece of wood and get to the food. He concluded from this that learning was a gradual and incremental process that was controlled by reward.

Edward Thorndike discovered that learning could be controlled by reward through his puzzle box.

Skinner box

Skinner Box

The Skinner box comprises a chamber in which has been placed a small animal (usually a pigeon or a white rat). In the chamber there is either a lever for rats to press or a key for pigeons to peck. The lever or key is connected to a food hopper. When the lever or key is depressed or pecked, food is released and made available to the animal. The experimenter sets the number and timing of lever presses or key pecks necessary to release food from the hopper. Lever presses or key pecks are recorded on a revolving roll of paper to produce a cumulative record of the animal's behaviour.

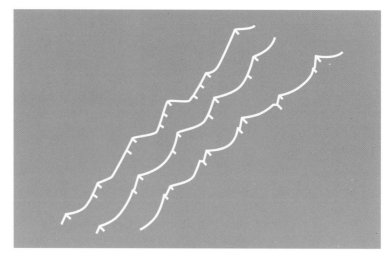

Above is the cumulative frequency response. The three curves come from studies on very different organisms. They represent a pigeon, a dog and a rat respectively.

OPERANT CONDITIONING

OPERANT CONDITIONING ▶ *the use of positive and negative reinforcement to change behaviour.*

After extensive experimentation, Skinner came to the conclusion that he had discovered qualitatively different principles of learning from those reported by Pavlov. He named the type of learning he had demonstrated in the Skinner Box as *Operant Conditioning*. In this kind of learning, the experimental animal 'operated' on the environment rather than simply responding to it. The crucial feature of Operant Conditioning is that learning is dependent on the response of the organism. In Skinner's terminology, behaviour is *emitted* by an organism. If the frequency of occurrence of this behaviour changes over time (its response strength) we say that this behaviour is being *reinforced*.

For a hungry person, food is positively reinforcing.

When we are hungry we exhibit behaviour that we hope will lead to the consumption of food. Food is **positively reinforcing** for a hungry person. If we are sated the sight of food does not increase food consumption behaviour so in this case food is not a **reinforcer**. Skinner had no place for concepts that he considered mentalistic or subjective in his work, so to talk about whether an animal has feelings of 'hunger' is actually misleading. After all, we cannot ask a pigeon or rat if they are hungry! Instead Skinner operationalised what we, in our everyday language, call hunger as being, for example, 70 per cent of average body weight. After an experiment was over, the rat or pigeon would be ready for further experimentation only once it had been deprived of food long enough for its body weight to return to the 70-per-cent level.

Positive reinforcement

This table shows the different types of reinforcement identified by Skinner and different schedules (patterns) of reinforcement and their consequences for changing behaviour.

Types of Reinforcement and Examples

- **Positive reinforcement**
  Add a rewarding stimulus (work hard and receive a pay rise).
- **Negative reinforcement**
  Remove an aversive stimulus (work hard and remove threat of redundancy).
- **Positive punishment**
  Add an aversive stimulus (slack at work and be handed more work to finish).
- **Negative punishment**
  Remove a rewarding stimulus (slack at work and be required to work through lunch).

Schedules of Reinforcement and Examples

Continuous reinforcement
Every piece of behaviour produces an effect.

Intermittent reinforcement
- Fixed ratio piece work (reinforcer produced after a set number of responses).
- Fixed interval hourly wage (reinforcer produced after a set period of time).
- Variable ratio slot machine (reinforcer produced after an average number of responses).
- Variable interval spot checks (reinforcer produced after an average time interval).

Skinner used pigeons to demonstrate the power of operant conditioning.

Reinforcement and Shaping Behaviour

Skinner repeatedly demonstrated the power of Operant Conditioning. He reported the example of one of his pigeons who had been on a variable ratio schedule of reinforcement. It continued to make 73,000 responses over a period of 4.5 hours after reinforcement was discontinued and the response was *extinguished*. He also demonstrated the power of operant conditioning by demonstrating how complex behaviours could be trained through the application of positive reinforcement.

SHAPING ▶ *the use of reinforcement to perform more and more specific behaviours.*

Skinner's rat Pliny was taught by a process of *shaping* (the use of reinforcement to perform more and more specific behaviours). He was then able to execute a complex string of behaviours: '...pulling a string to obtain a marble from a rack, picking the marble up with the forepaws, lifting it to the top of the tube, and dropping it inside'. Every step in the process had to be worked out through a series of approximations, since the component responses were not in the original repertoire of the rat (1938, p. 340).

Shaping

As with Watson before him, Skinner's ambition was to provide an approach that covered all psychology and also, as Watson before him, to rid psychology of anything that smacked of the mental, private and subjective. For Skinner, the kind of shaping demonstrated when Pliny picked up the marble and dropped it down a tube was no different from the processes that result in us being able to read a book, fly a plane or paint a picture. He believed humans are born with more sophisticated bodies and a greater repertoire of behaviour that we can display but the process of operant conditioning is the same across the animal kingdom.

Skinner went as far as to write a book called *Beyond Freedom and Dignity* (1971) in which he argued that ideas such as autonomy and emancipation, when used to organise human societies, had produced more distress than happiness. They should be replaced by organization based on suitably designed schedules of reinforcement.

Conditioning and society

In a work of science fiction, *Walden Two* (1948), he described a Utopian society based on operant conditioning in which the direction and growth of the community was the result of continual behavioural experimentation. Behaviours and routines that increased overall cohesion and well-being were abandoned. Crucial to Skinner's vision was that the growth and the development of the community was not based on complex assumtpions about human nature, but basically on the pragmatic principle of trial and error.

Behaviourism in Psychology

While it is true to say that there has never been a consensus about theories and methods in psychology, the nearest to consensus that was ever achieved was from the end of the 1930s until the late 1950s and early 1960s when Behaviourism was the dominant approach to psychology. During this time, social psychologists (see Chapter 6), personality psychologists (see Chapter 8), developmental psychologists (see Chapter 5) and differential psychologists tried to couch their work in terms of stimulus and response. The grip of behaviourism was loosened when cognitive psychologists began to reintroduce concepts such as memory and attention that were intrinsically mental (see Chapter 2). One of the key moments in the rise of cognitive psychology and fall of behaviourism was in 1959 when the linguist Noam Chomsky argued that Skinner's account of the child's development of language could not be understood as the result of Operant Conditioning. According to Chomsky, the 'lexical explosion' or rapid increase in vocabulary in the first few years of life was so great that it could not be explained in terms of learning the relations between stimulus and response. For Chomsky, children can learn so many new words so quickly because concepts are innate and not learned at all.

Wolfgang Köhler founded Gestalt Psychology, which explained our conscious experience as a dynamic whole.

NAMES TO KNOW: GESTALT PSYCHOLOGY

Max Wertheimer *(1880–1943)*

Kurt Koffka *(1886–1941)*

Wolfgang Köhler *(1887–1967)*

OTHER APPROACHES TO LEARNING: GESTALT PSYCHOLOGY

Wolfgang Köhler (1887–1967) was one of the founders of Gestalt Psychology, along with Max Wertheimer (1880–1943) and Kurt Koffka (1886–1941). They developed Gestalt Psychology as an alternative to the introspective psychology of Wundt, which we looked at in the first chapter. Their problem with Wundt was that he insisted on breaking down consciousness into elements.

APPERCEPTION ▶ *a mental process that stitches the elements back together as a conscious experience.*

The *gestaltists*, in contrast, argued that our conscious experience did not come to us as elements that had to be, as it were, stuck back together through a process Wundt called *apperception* but that our experience is always organised as part of a dynamic whole or *gestalt*. Beginning with visual stimuli, they identified a number of principles of gestalt organisation. The gestaltists believed that our

Gestalt organisation

GESTALT ▶ *our experience is organised as part of a dynamic whole.*

experience is ordered into gestalts because the world itself is structured as sets of physical fields. They believed that there was an 'isomorphism' (a similarity of structure) between the physical world, the brain and our behaviour.

Behaviourism in Psychology
The diagram to the right illustrates five of these principles. In the top line we see the grey circles as a set of four pairs because the members of each 'pair' are slightly closer together than the next 'pair' of circles. This illustrates the principal of proximity. In the second row we group items that resemble one another. This illustrates the principle of similarity. In the third row we put the pairs of brackets together and see four partial squares rather than eight single lines with upper and lower bars. This illustrates the principle of closure. In the fourth line we see the diagram on the left as two crossed lines and the diagram on the right as two discrete shapes. The only difference is that in the first the shapes are touching and in the second they are separate. This illustrates the principle of good continuation. In the fourth row the pairs are grouped because they occupy a common region of space (the shaded region). This illustrates the principle of common region.

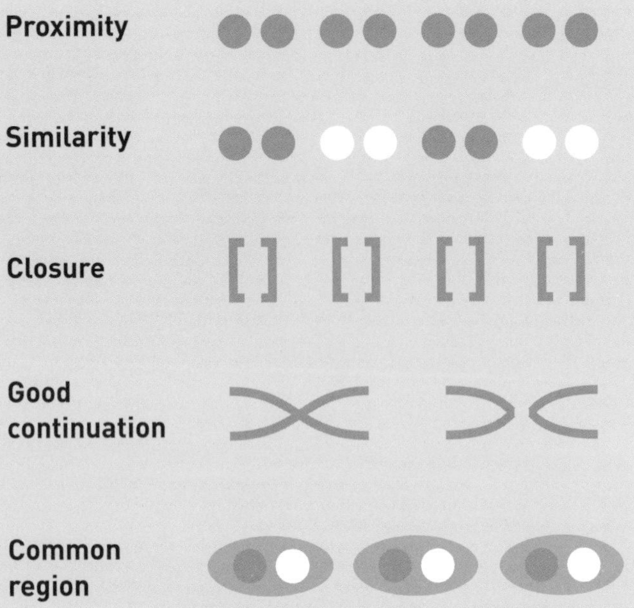

Proximity

Similarity

Closure

Good continuation

Common region

Animal learning

WOLFGANG KÖHLER AND THE ANTHROPOID RESEARCH STATION AT TENERIFE

In 1913, Wolfgang Köhler was appointed director of a research station at Tenerife, in the Canary Islands. The goal of the research station was to investigate the natural biological bases of individual and social morality by studying chimpanzees and other apes. Shortly after Köhler arrived in the Canary Islands, the First World War broke out and Köhler was stranded at the research station for the duration of the war.

As we have seen, Pavlov and Skinner believed that the principles of learning applied across the animal kingdom. It was more convenient to experiment on dogs, rats and pigeons because they bred quickly and fitted quite nicely into boxes or harnesses! Köhler's animals were chimpanzees and orangutans, species that were much closer in evolutionary terms to us than our four-legged or two-legged friends. When he set his experimental participants problems to solve, he identified learning principles very different from those of Pavlovian and Operant Conditioning.

What is a Gestalt?

Try this simple demonstration for yourself. Hum a simple melody: 'Baa Baa Black Sheep' or 'Mary Had a Little Lamb', for example. Now whistle the same tune. Change the key by whistling the tune in a higher register or humming in a low bass growl. Imagine the melody played by the different instruments of a symphony orchestra: a reedy piccolo or a deep bassoon. Even the least musical among us can produce the same melody with different pitches and we can slow down or speed up our tune and still recognise the melody. According to gestalt psychologists, a melody is an example of a gestalt. It is a structured whole that can be transformed in various ways but its structure remains. This illustrates what Koffka said about gestalts:

> 'It has been said: The whole is more than the sum of its parts. It is more correct to say that the whole is something else than the sum of its parts, because summing up is a meaningless procedure, whereas the whole–part relationship is meaningful.' (Kurt Koffka, *Principles of Gestalt Psychology* (1935)

'...what is given me by the melody does not arise ... as a secondary process from the sum of the pieces as such. Instead, what takes place in each single part already depends upon what the whole is.' (1925/1938) In other words, one hears the melody first and only then may perceptually divide it up into notes.

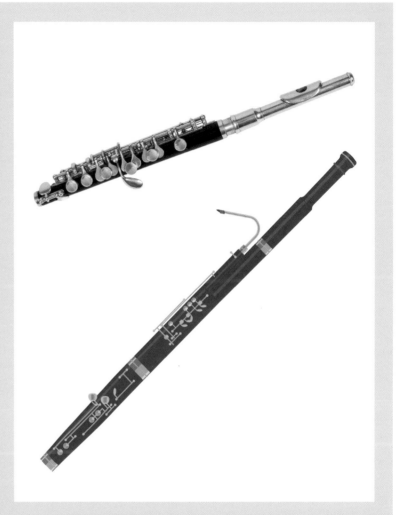

A tune like 'Mary Had a Little Lamb' sounds different when played on a piccolo or a bassoon – an example of how a structured whole can be transformed in different ways, but its essential structure remains.

*Comparative
approach to learning*

The kinds of problems that Köhler set for his apes needed for their solution the negotiation of detours (going away from a goal in order to eventually reach it), using tools and even making tools. The Pavlovian and Skinnerian approaches regarded learning as a gradual process – the result of the passive association of US and CS, or the association of emitted response and reinforcing stimulus. Thorndike demonstrated a similar approach with his Puzzle Boxes. Köhler, on the other hand, understood learning (or better problem solving) to be the result of gestalt reorganization and insight – a thoroughly mental concept.

Köhler's approach to learning was *comparative*, that is, he did not expect all animals to learn in the same way and was interested in identifying commonalities and *differences* in animal intelligence. In one particularly illuminating study, Köhler compared the way two very different animals, a chicken and a chimpanzee, set about the task of trying to retrieve food that had been placed behind a barrier. For Köhler, what was crucial about these two was that the chicken's path was gradual and tentative whereas the chimpanzee's path was smooth and continuous. In Köhler terms, the chimpanzee had grasped the geography of the environment and the solution to the problem as a gestalt and, without trial or error, grasped the solution to the problem. In other experiments, Köhler noted that when his chimpanzees were presented with a problem they spent time simply looking around before tackling it. It was as if they were sizing up the situation before acting.

This wasn't to say that the chimpanzees always solved the problems they were presented with but that the way they approached the problem was different from those taken by rats and pigeons. The mistakes that the apes made in solving the problems he had set them suggested that they had misunderstood the problem or were simply mechanically reproducing solutions that had worked on other tasks. In Chapter 5, when we look at developmental psychology, we will examine work with children that follows in this tradition and focuses on examining mistakes as clues to making sense of conceptual understanding. After the end of the war, Köhler returned to Germany, where he abandoned further work with chimpanzees and orangutans, because their high intelligence, which made them so interesting, also made them rather difficult and challenging research participants.

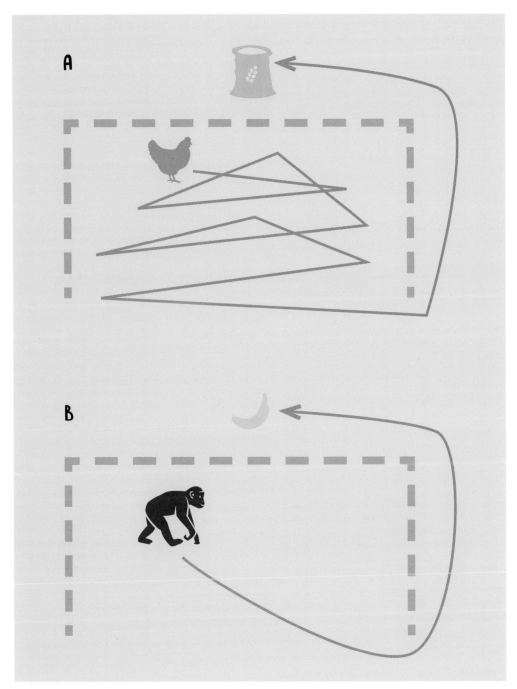

This diagram shows Kohler's detour experiments. (A) shows the path taken by a chicken to reach food placed behind a barrier, and (B) shows the path taken by a chimpanzee to reach food placed behind a barrier.

Sultan the Chimpanzee and the Banana

In one experiment involving Sultan the chimpanzee, Köhler suspended a banana from a hook hanging from the roof of the animal enclosure. The banana was too high for the chimpanzee to reach, so Sultan first spent time looking at the wooden boxes in the enclosure and then arranged them as a tower that he could climb and thus reach the prize. This was one of Köhler's celebrated examples of insight learning that demonstrated that the chimpanzees were capable of mentally coming up with novel solutions to problems they had not encountered before and could not be understood as the result of trial and error learning.

In a second experiment, a banana was placed outside the bars of the chimpanzee enclosure beyond Sultan's reach. The banana was also too far away to reach with one of the sticks that were lying around. After some time playing, Sultan discovered that the end of one stick could be pushed into the end of the other making a longer stick. With this new long stick he could reach the banana. Whenever presented with this problem, Sultan would immediately fit two sticks together and gain his treat.

Sultan the Chimpanzee created a ladder out of wooden boxes to reach a banana hanging from the roof.

SUMMARY

In the mid-twentieth century the Behaviourists proposed that the study of associative learning should be the model for the study of all psychological phenomena. Their dream of a unified psychology underpinned the principles of Classical and Operant Conditioning did not come to pass. The principles of learning demonstrated by Pavlov with his dogs, Thorndike with his cats and Skinner with his rats and pigeons proved to be robust and easily replicated. Skinner's followers elaborated on his findings and learnt more and more about the complexities of schedules of reinforcement. However, observations of the learning of orangutans and chimpanzees by Köhler and of human problem solving by his gestalt colleagues as well as the work of the cognitive psychologists which we will turn to in the next chapter, showed that associative learning was not the complete explanation of intelligent behaviour and a means of understanding all aspects of the psychological realm.

In the final analysis how rats and pigeons learn is an important question in its own right, but there are important differences between organisms that should not be overlooked. The radical suggestion made by both Watson and Skinner that the very concept of the mental and any concepts that allude to the mental including 'hoping', 'wishing', 'wanting', 'thinking' and so forth proved to be a step too far for both the public and psychologists and the concept of the mind has never been exorcised from our vocabulary.

Nevertheless, the contribution of the Behaviourists should still be acknowledged. They forced psychologists who rejected their key claims to think carefully about how mental phenomena could be studied scientifically and they also were responsible for inventing a range of techniques based on reinforcement and shaping that are still used to change behaviour today. In Chapter 9, we will learn how clinicians married behavioural techniques with principles drawn from cognitive psychology (see Chapter 3) to produce *Cognitive Behavioural Therapy* which is used extensively to treat depression and anxiety. Today there are few psychologists who would describe themselves as Behaviourists, but all psychologists study learning theory and understand the importance of associative learning.

THE HISTORY OF PSYCHOLOGY

THE PSYCHOLOGY OF LEARNING

The British empiricists argued that truth and certainty could not be gained by looking inside ourselves. The mind itself was, in John Locke's (1632–1704) phrase, a tabula rasa (or 'blank slate') on which experience was written. David Hume (1711–76) argued that there were no ideas in our minds that were not given by experience. To avoid error, we must trace our ideas back to the experiences that produced them. When one billiard ball strikes another we expect the struck billiard to move away. We do so because we have experienced this before and have learned to expect the connection through a process of association or habit. In the nineteenth century, Ivan Pavlov (1849–1936) empirically studied learning by association in the laboratory and demonstrated the principles of what we now know of as 'Classical' or 'Pavlovian Conditioning', in which a stimulus that leads to a reflex action is substituted with a new stimulus.

J.B. Watson (1878–1958) proposed to make this kind of conditioning the basis of all psychology. Edward Thorndike (1874–1949) showed that associations were made not just between stimuli but also by a response and its consequences. This new type of associative learning was further developed by B.F. Skinner (1904–90), who proposed his theory of *Operant Conditioning*. These behaviourist approaches dominated psychology from the 1920s to 1960s, when they were challenged by cognitive psychologists drawing on the principles of information processing. The behaviourist principles of learning have been found to be robust but they cannot explain all learning. The gestalt psychologists, Max Wertheimer (1880–1943), Kurt Koffka (1886–1941) and Wolfgang Köhler (1887–1967), argued that problem-solving could not be understood as the result of simple associative learning and proposed that learning involved the reorganisation of an 'organised whole' called the *gestalt*.

Ivan Pavlov discovered the principles of classical conditioning through his laboratory experiments.

Chapter Three

COGNITIVE PSYCHOLOGY

Information and the Mind – Cognitive Psychology – Experimental Studies – Memory and Meaning – Primacy and Recency – Cognition and Computers – Levels of Processing – Working Memory Model – Other Approaches

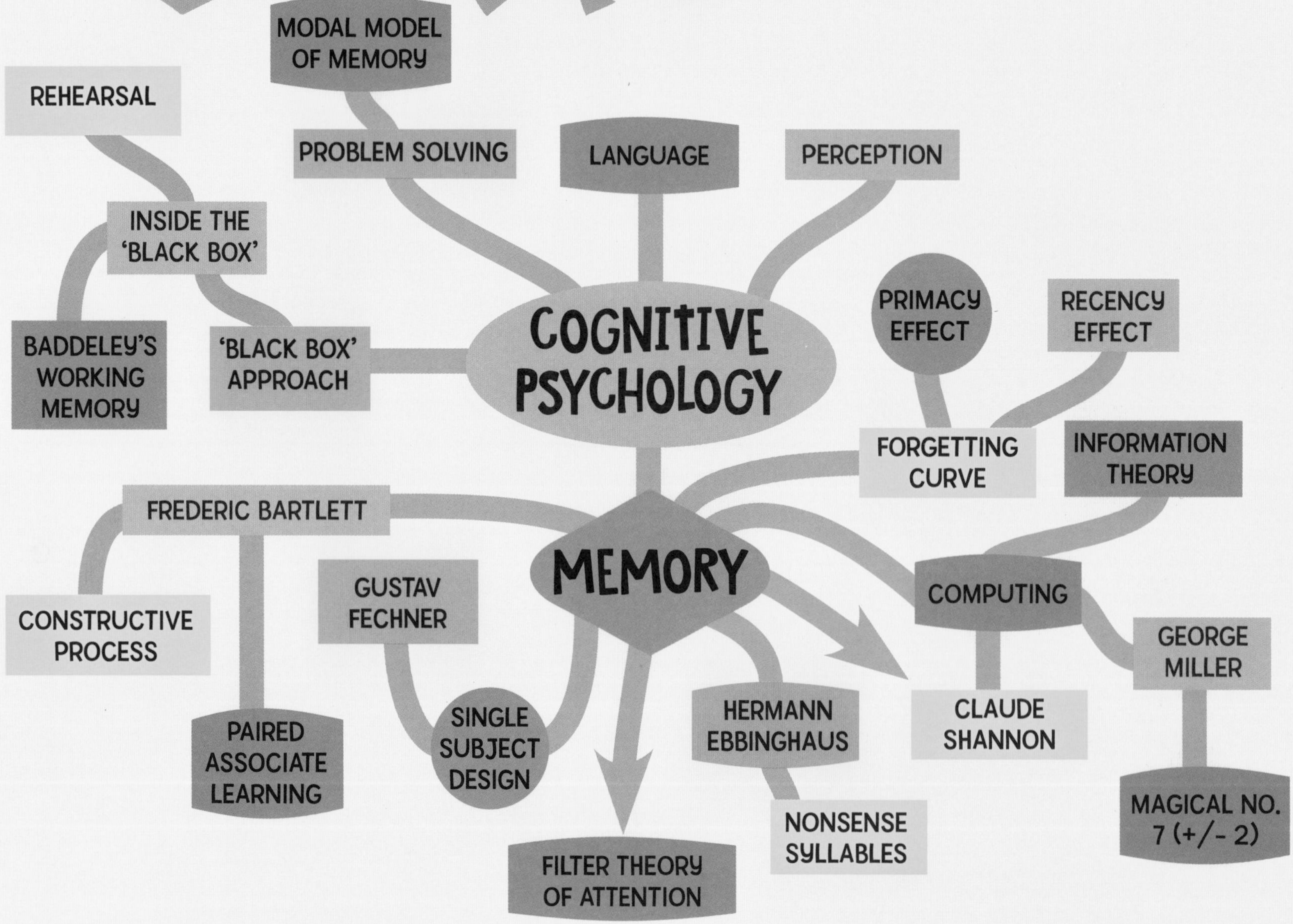

MODAL MODEL OF MEMORY
REHEARSAL
PROBLEM SOLVING
LANGUAGE
PERCEPTION
INSIDE THE 'BLACK BOX'
BADDELEY'S WORKING MEMORY
'BLACK BOX' APPROACH
COGNITIVE PSYCHOLOGY
PRIMACY EFFECT
RECENCY EFFECT
FORGETTING CURVE
INFORMATION THEORY
FREDERIC BARTLETT
MEMORY
COMPUTING
CONSTRUCTIVE PROCESS
GUSTAV FECHNER
GEORGE MILLER
SINGLE SUBJECT DESIGN
HERMANN EBBINGHAUS
CLAUDE SHANNON
PAIRED ASSOCIATE LEARNING
NONSENSE SYLLABLES
MAGICAL NO. 7 (+/- 2)
FILTER THEORY OF ATTENTION

INFORMATION AND THE MIND

I can sit in my chair and summon up an image of a unicorn. I can construct stories about my unicorn and imagine a whole world for the unicorn to roam. I might sit down at my laptop and represent these flights of fancy and images in words and, maybe have them published in a book so that other people can look at the text on the page and share my world. In a few weeks' time, you might recall reading about unicorns when you are talking with a friend about the psychology of thinking. All the activities I have described are the subject matter of *cognitive psychology*, which studies how information is encoded, stored, manipulated and transmitted in order to model and explain the functioning of the human mind.

Imagining a unicorn, writing about a unicorn and remembering reading about a unicorn are all activities covered by the subject of cognitive psychology.

OF THE VNICORNE.

THE RISE OF COGNITIVE PSYCHOLOGY

Cognitive psychology became an important area of psychology in its own right in the 1960s. Before then, topics that we think of as essentially cognitive had been studied in a rather piecemeal manner. During the heyday of behaviourism, they were usually explained in terms of the learning principles of association between stimulus and response, as described in the previous chapter.

Researching memory   Cognitive psychology as an experimental science that takes the mental of the cognitive realm seriously can be traced back to early research on memory.

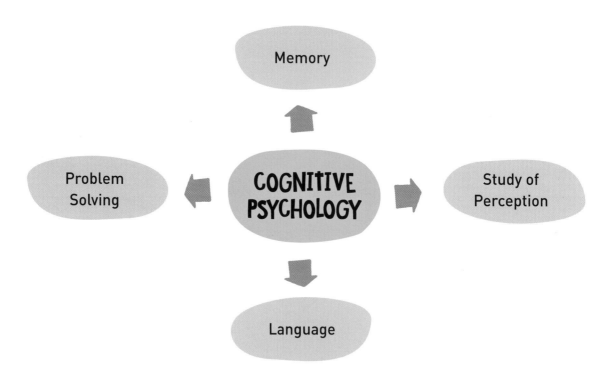

Cognitive psychology includes, among other areas, the study of perception, problem solving and language. So it is impossible to do justice to the full scope of the subject in a single short chapter. To illustrate the basic methods and theories of cognitive psychology, we will begin by looking at where it all began: memory.

EXPERIMENTAL STUDIES OF MEMORY

Gustav Fechner invented *psychophysics* to demonstrate the reality of the mental realm (see page 66) and, in the process, invented a new science. He chose to study simple perceptual judgements, such as the discrimination of weight, experimenting on himself in a methodology that today we call a single subject design.

Gustav Fechner

SINGLE SUBJECT DESIGN ▶ *an experiment in which the subject serves as his/her own control.*

Fechner's findings and methodological rigour as a means of studying the mental realm inspired Hermann Ebbinghaus (1850–1909) to develop related methods to investigate higher cognitive functions. What fascinated Ebbinghaus was how we learn and remember people, events and objects: human memory. What made human memory a tricky area to study compared to simple perceptual judgements was that the objects involved in remembering, say, a phone number from yesterday or one's first kiss many years ago have very different significance and memorability. Ebbinghaus published his research in a book *Memory: A Contribution to Experimental Psychology* (1885).

Nonsense Syllables

Ebbinghaus addressed the potentially confounding influence of previous experience by inventing nonsense syllables. These were three-letter combinations of consonants and vowels (for example 'bok' and 'lov') that had no intrinsic meaning and were therefore neither more nor less memorable than each other. Experimenting on himself, Ebbinghaus investigated how many times he had to repeat a list (he called a list a 'series') of nonsense syllables before he could recall the series perfectly in the right order. He found that the longer the series the more repetitions were necessary to learn it. He also discovered that it was much more effective to space apart the practice sessions than try to learn the lot in one go. This finding has been shown to be robust and useful in designing revision schedules. Don't wait until just before an exam to cram as much information as possible. Learn material in small batches as you go along and you will remember much more!

Series

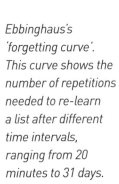

Repetition and learning

Forgetting Curves

As well as investigating the learning of lists, he also investigated forgetting. After about 20 minutes Ebbinghaus could no longer remember the list perfectly. However, to learn the list again needed about 40 per cent fewer repetitions than when he first learned it. The more repetitions needed to relearn the list is an index of forgetting. As time between learning the first list increases, the number of repetitions needed to learn the list again goes up and the percentage of memory saved is less and less. Crucially, though, something is always remembered. In Ebbinghaus's experiments, forgetting was never forever.

Ebbinghaus's 'forgetting curve'. This curve shows the number of repetitions needed to re-learn a list after different time intervals, ranging from 20 minutes to 31 days.

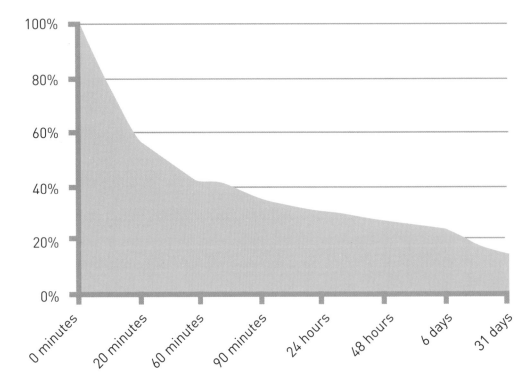

Primacy and Recency Effects

One important phenomenon he noticed was that when he was learning his series of nonsense syllables the words at the beginning and ends of the series were more easily learned than the words in the middle. The better learning or recall at the beginning is known as the ***primacy effect*** and the better recall at the end is called the finality or ***recency effect***.

PRIMACY EFFECT ▶ *recall is better for items at the beginning of a list.*

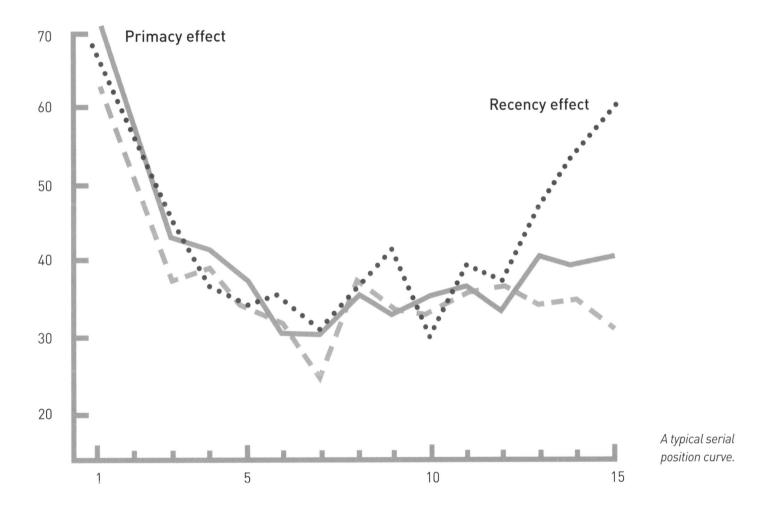

Primacy effect

Recency effect

A typical serial position curve.

RECENCY EFFECT ▶ *recall is better for items at the end of the list.*

The 'Black Box' approach. Behaviourists refused to address what went on between stimulus and response. Cognitive psychology developed when researchers began to think of what went on between input and output in terms of information processing.

INSIDE THE BLACK BOX

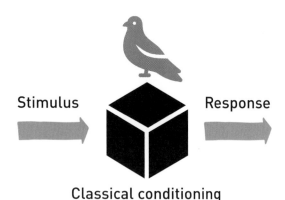

Stimulus   Response

Classical conditioning

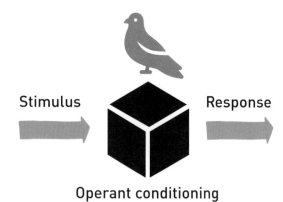

Stimulus   Response

Operant conditioning

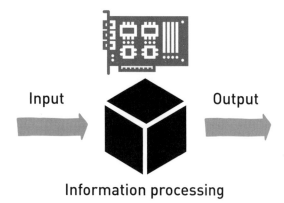

Input   Output

Information processing

The Verbal Learning Tradition

Ebbinghaus had invented a methodology – serial learning – and had discovered some key characteristics of how we learn material. These were that it is better to space out practice than try to learn material all at once, and that memory of a subject matter drops off but never fully disappears. In the context of behaviourism, his findings were interpreted as a contribution to verbal learning and the investigation of the association between being presented with verbal stimuli and verbal responses. However, behaviourists believed that going 'inside the box' was pure speculation and they were not concerned whether the relationship between stimulus and response was studied using rats, pigeons or people. As we shall see later, cognitive psychologists were more willing to go 'inside the black box' and think about 'the box' in terms of a digital computer (see page 54).

MEMORY AND MEANING

Ebbinghaus invented nonsense syllables in order to produce a supply of material that could be learned and subsequently remembered without being affected by previous learning. At the University of Cambridge in the 1930s, Sir Frederic Bartlett (1886–1969) designed a study based on very different premises. His interest wasn't the number of nonsense syllables correctly recalled but how new information is taken in and subsequently remembered. In 1932, he published *Remembering: A Study in Experimental and Social Psychology*. Compared with the verbal learning tradition, Bartlett's approach was very different. He shifted the focus from the recall of material that was intentionally devoid of meaning, to the process of remembering stories that were the product of different cultures. These were stories that could only be fully understood if the reader was at home in that culture. The material he chose for his studies of remembering was drawn from Amerindian folktales and his participants were students who knew nothing of them. Their problem was to make sense of the story. Participants were asked to read through the story a couple of times at their usual reading speed and then, after a quarter of an hour, recount the story.

> ### NAMES TO KNOW:
> ### MEMORY RESEARCHERS
>
> *Hermann Ebbinghaus* (1850–1909)
>
> *Frederic Bartlett* (1886–1969)
>
> *Ulric Neisser* (1928–2012)

Stories and culture

Sir Frederic Bartlett (right) receives the Queen's Medal from the president of the Royal Society in 1952 for his work on memory.

Bartlett found that his students forgot elements they did not understand from the Native American folktale he used for his experiment.

War of the Ghosts

One night two young men from Egulac went down to the river to hunt seals and while they were there it became foggy and calm. Then they heard war-cries, and they thought: 'Maybe this is a war-party'. They escaped to the shore, and hid behind a log. Now canoes came up, and they heard the noise of paddles, and saw one canoe coming up to them. There were five men in the canoe, and they said: 'What do you think? We wish to take you along. We are going up the river to make war on the people.' One of the young men said, 'I have no arrows.' 'Arrows are in the canoe,' they said. 'I will not go along. I might be killed. My relatives do not know where I have gone. But you,' he said, turning to the other, 'may go with them.' So one of the young men went, but the other returned home.

And the warriors went on up the river to a town on the other side of Kalama. The people came down to the water and they began to fight, and many were killed. But presently the young man heard one of the warriors say, 'Quick, let us go home: that Indian has been hit.' Now he thought: 'Oh, they are ghosts.' He did not feel sick, but they said he had been shot.

So the canoes went back to Egulac and the young man went ashore to his house and made a fire. And he told everybody and said: 'Behold I accompanied the ghosts, and we went to fight. Many of our fellows were killed, and many of those who attacked us were killed. They said I was hit, and I did not feel sick.'

He told it all, and then he became quiet. When the sun rose he fell down. Something black came out of his mouth. His face became contorted. The people jumped up and cried.

He was dead.

Extract from Frederic Bartlett, *Remembering: A Study in Experimental and Social Psychology* (Cambridge University Press, 1932)

Remembering as a Construction

What Bartlett found was that his 20 participants omitted details they didn't understand (the supernatural elements) and added details to make the story they recounted more cogent. For Bartlett, this demonstrated that memory was more than simply recall and was, crucially, part of a *constructive process* that started with one's previous experiences, expectations and cultural knowledge.

Constructive process

Memory Forgotten

PAIRED ASSOCIATE LEARNING ▶ *a method in which a stimulus word and a response are paired together.*

Bartlett's alternative approach to remembering had limited influence. The dominant research tradition relied on the use of nonsense syllables or other methods such as paired associate learning, which requires a participant to respond to a stimulus word item with a different word. For example, when presented with the word 'cat' the participant is required to respond with the word 'pineapple'. These experiments were carried out, not under the rubric of memory, but of 'verbal learning'. The language of stimulus–response outlined in Chapter 2 had no place for mental terms for memory or remembering so they were replaced by stimulus, response and association.

Paired associate learning

COGNITION AND COMPUTERS

INFORMATION THEORY ▶ *treating a human as a communication channel through which data is transmitted as binary digits.*

Towards the end of the 1950s and into the 1960s, the grip of stimulus–response vocabulary began to loosen. George A. Miller (1920–2012) was influenced by the newly formulated *information theory* of Claude Shannon. Published in 1948, this regarded humans as *communication channels* and the data transported through the channel to be binary digits (0s or 1s) or bits.

Communication channels

To begin to understand the concept of information, think about this problem: if we were asked to put a single chess piece on a chess board and not let a friend see where it was, how many 'yes' or 'no' questions would they have to ask us in order to locate the piece? If we were to take each square individually we would potentially have to ask 64 questions to locate the piece. Things become easier if we recast the problem in terms of how many Yes/No questions we need to ask in order to solve the problem. It turns out that in a problem that has a potential of 64 answers, the answer is six because $2×2×2×2×2×2 = 64$.

Try this for yourself:

- Is the chess piece in the top or bottom half of the board?

- Left or right half of the remainder of the board?

- Top or bottom half of that remainder?

- Left or right half of what is left?

- Upper or lower of the two squares remaining?

The Magical Number Seven

Miller borrowed a new vocabulary from Shannon. Instead of *stimulus*, *response*, *association* and *reinforcement*, he talked about *channels*, *information*, *capacity* and *coding*.

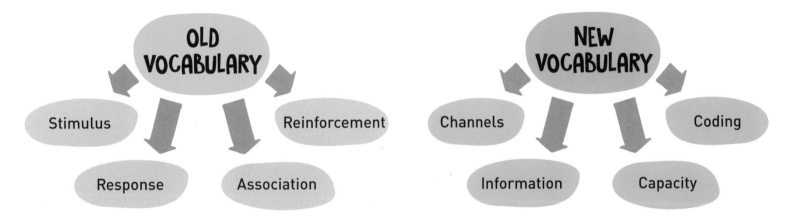

Reviewing the research on sensory judgements and memory, he pointed to similarities in results irrespective of whether the stimuli being studied were auditory, visual or strings of numbers. Again and again different researchers had found that an individual can discriminate between five and nine tones of different pitch, loudness, lengths of lines and number of digits recalled. In his 1956 paper 'The Magical Number Seven, Plus or Minus Two: Some Limits on Our Capacity for Processing Information', he explained these results in terms of the capacity of the human mind to process information as being limited to about seven plus or minus two items or 2.6 bits of information. This channel capacity explains why most of us have difficulty remembering phone numbers that are longer than seven digits.

Discriminating tones

Of course we can remember some phone numbers that are much longer. My own phone number has 11 digits. Can I remember this number because I have a superior memory? According to Miller this is not the case. The channel capacity is limited to 2.6 bits of information but it is the information capacity that is limited – not the number of raw digits. By 'chunking' numbers together, I (and everyone else) can reduce the amount of information in the system. For example, put together the first four digits that make up the area code to make 1 bit of information and gathers the rest of the number into a group of four and a group of three digits.

AREA CODE	INFORMATION GROUP ONE	INFORMATION GROUP TWO
0209	3579	246

MEMORY RECONSIDERED

Computer memory model

Thinking about cognitive phenomena in terms of processing bits of information led researchers to reconsider theories of memory. The verbal learning tradition, with its focus on association, was largely abandoned and new ways of conceptualising memory were proposed. In 1968, Atkinson and Shiffrin explored the computer as a useful analogy for memory and were unapologetic about going inside the 'black box', distinguishing between memory structures and control processes. The memory structures were the equivalent of computer hardware and the boot programs that run automatically when we switch on a computer. The control processes are the operations that we can set in motion by launching a program or application.

NAMES TO KNOW: MODELLERS OF MEMORY

Donald Broadbent *(1926–93)*

Richard Atkinson *(1929–present)*

George A. Miller *(1920–2012)*

Alan Baddeley *(1934–present)*

Richard Shiffrin *(1942–present)*

Richard Atkinson developed the modal model of memory along with Richard Shiffrin.

MODAL MODEL THEORY OF MEMORY ▶ *memory is made up of sensory memory, short-term memory and long-term memory.*

Atkinson and Shiffrin proposed the *modal model theory of memory*. This model proposes that memory is made up of a sensory store that can contain information directly from the senses for a short period of time. For example, as Miller had pointed out, short-term memory maps have the capacity of seven plus or minus two chunks of information (see page 53) and this information can be retained if it is *rehearsed*.

REHEARSAL ▶ *the process of storing information in short-term memory by repetition.*

Rehearsal is a process of maintaining the contents of the *short-term memory* (STM) by, for example, saying the digits of a phone number again and again. Material that is rehearsed is translated to *long-term memory* (LTM) where it may be retrieved. This nicely explains the primacy/recency effect discussed earlier. Material that is presented at the start of the list is practised or rehearsed more so is more likely to pass in to LTM. Material at the end of the list remains in STM so can easily be recalled when asked.

The Modal Model of Memory after Atkinson and Shiffrin (1968)

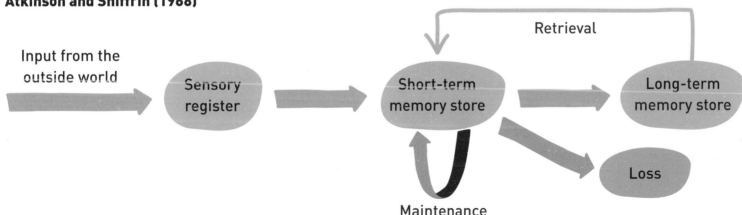

Levels of Processing

Whilst the multi-store model of memory, comprising of a number of discrete stores, was attractive and fitted in well with the conception of cognition as an information processing task run on a digital computer, other models were also developed. Craik and Lockhart in 1972 published a highly influential paper which drew attention not so much on where memories were stored but on how material was initially processed. They found that the instructions given to experimental participants lead to better or worse recall. Directing participants to the case of a word e.g. look to see if it is written 'cat' or 'Cat' or if a pair of words rhyme like 'pig' and 'wig' lead to less recall than if participants were asked to think about the meaning of the word. According to Craik and Lockhart, recall was related to the depth of processing with attending to meaning leading to deep processing and superior recall and attending to surface features of the word (capital or lower case letter) requiring only shallow processing and leading to poor recall. Craik and Lockhart's experimental findings are robust (easy to replicate), but their theory of levels of processing although intuitively appealing is difficult to specify precisely because we have no independent measure of the depth of processing. Semantic processing appears to be in some way 'deeper' than processing the shape of letters, but it is not clear how this is the case. We will now turn to a theory of memory which builds on the Multi Modal Model but proposes that short-term memory is much more complex than Atkinson and Shiffren supposed.

Colin Cherry discovered the 'Cocktail Party effect' in 1953, where we can zone out background noise and hold our attention in a conversation with friends.

ATTENTION

Psychologists from Wundt onward had been concerned with the problem of attention. How is it possible that in a busy and demanding environment we can switch our focus to different areas within our conscious experience? As well as the theoretical problem of what this tells us about the nature of consciousness it is also a practical problem for people working in noisy and complex environments such as on the flight deck of an aeroplane or for a military radio operator in battle.

In 1953 Colin Cherry was researching the problem of attention and distraction. He noted that at a party, despite the general hubbub, we manage to hold a conversation with a couple of friends while zoning out background music, other conversations and the clink of glasses. He called this the **Cocktail Party Effect** and designed some experiments to investigate how it worked. The experimental paradigm was known as a **dichotic listening** task, in which a participant wears headphones and different messages are played to the left and the right ear at the same time.

Cocktail party effect

In one experimental elaboration called **shadowing** the listener is asked to attend to the message coming in one particular ear and repeat the message aloud as he or she hears it. What Cherry found was that if one focuses on the message coming through one ear, the message coming through the other ear does not register. One can report that the message was from a man or a woman, loud or quiet but not the content.

Shadowing

BROADBENT'S INFORMATION PROCESSING MODEL OF COGNITION

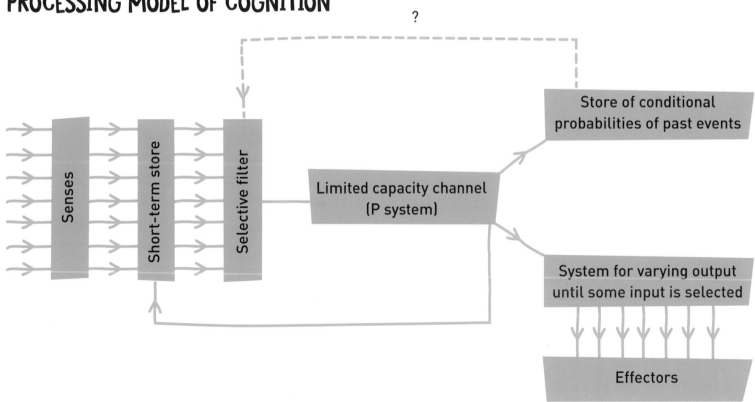

FILTER THEORY OF ATTENTION ▶ *everything we sense passes through a 'filter' that only admits signals with the right properties.*

In 1958, in his book *Perception and Communication*, Donald Broadbent (1926–1993) developed an explicitly information processing account of attention processes illustrated in the previous diagram. In this diagram sensory input is held in a short-term store and then passed through a selective filter. This selective filter is connected to the central limited-capacity channel which is the equivalent of a computer processor. The selective filter stops the processor from being overloaded by information. Selected information is processed through the limited capacity channel resulting in output or a change to the store of conditional probabilities which will change or keep the selective filter settings. Broadbent amended his model in the light of further experimental work by himself and by colleagues. It was highly influential in the development of cognitive psychology as it was one of the first, if not the first, explicit diagram illustrating the flow of information in a unified model of human information processing.

Other evidence for different kinds of memory
Henry Gustav Molaison (1926–2008) known to generations of psychology students under the pseudonym of H.M. was hit by a bicycle when he was nine years old. Afterwards he suffered from serious and distressing convulsions and seizures. When he was 27 years old as a treatment of last resort he underwent brain surgery to remove his hippocampus. The convulsions stopped but H.M.'s memory was left profoundly damaged. From the moment he woke up after the operation his ability to recount new experiences was profoundly impaired. He would not remember someone whom he had met 24 hours earlier. This provided evidence for the separation of short- and long-term memory. It seemed that for H.M. material in short term memory did not get passed on to long-term memory and he forgot anything that happened after about a 20-second period. It turned out that the picture was more complicated because although he couldn't remember practising and learning motor activities such as tracing the reflection of a five pointed star in a mirror his performance on this task improved over time. This lead to memory theorists making the distinction between ***declarative*** or ***explicit*** memory (what H.M. had lost) and ***implicit*** memory.

BADDELEY'S WORKING MEMORY MODEL

In 1974 Baddeley and Hitch introduced the theory of *Working Memory*. They argued that the Modal Model of Memory which situated the short-term memory between the Sensory Store and long-term memory was too simple to do justice to the data collected from memory experiments, observations of patients with memory loss and neuroscientific evidence. Conceptualising short-term memory as simply a store for information about events, words, names and digits did not do justice to the cognitive work which was done at this stage of processing. Baddeley and Hitch proposed replacing the concept of short-term memory with the concept of Working Memory.

WORKING MEMORY ▶ *short-term memory is where we think; it consists of three systems: the visuo-spatial sketchpad, the episodic buffer and the phonological loop.*

Working Memory was not a single unitary system but comprised of three inter-related subsystems; the central executive, the visuospatial sketch pad (VSSP) and the phonological loop. The Central Executive is responsible for controlling the encoding, storing and retrieval of information by the VSSP and the phonological loop. The Episodic Buffer allows temporary storage and integration of information from these components and also links to Episodic Memory. When we are actively problem solving the VSSP allows us to generate and manipulate visual images. The articulatory loop is made up of a phonological memory store that holds acoustic or speech based material and the articulatory subvocal loop that allows us to keep material in the phonological store. Without the use of the articulatory loop, material in the memory store would decay very quickly.

VSSP

In his book *Essentials of Human Memory* published in 1999, Baddeley suggests a simple exercise to illustrate working memory. Multiply 23 by 7 in your head. Don't look at the page and do the calculation. The answer is 161 and to get that answer you probably had to use the subvocal loop to keep the 23 and 7 in your mind or you may have visualised the numbers on the page. You would then multiply the 3 by 7 to get 21 and have to remember that you need to carry the two before you multiply the 2 by 7 to get 14 and add the carried 2 to get 16. The 16 goes in front of the 1 from the original 3 multiplied by 7 and the answer is 161! Even a simple calculation like 23 multiplied by 7 requires the allocation of memory resources by the central executive and the temporary storage of phonological information and visual information.

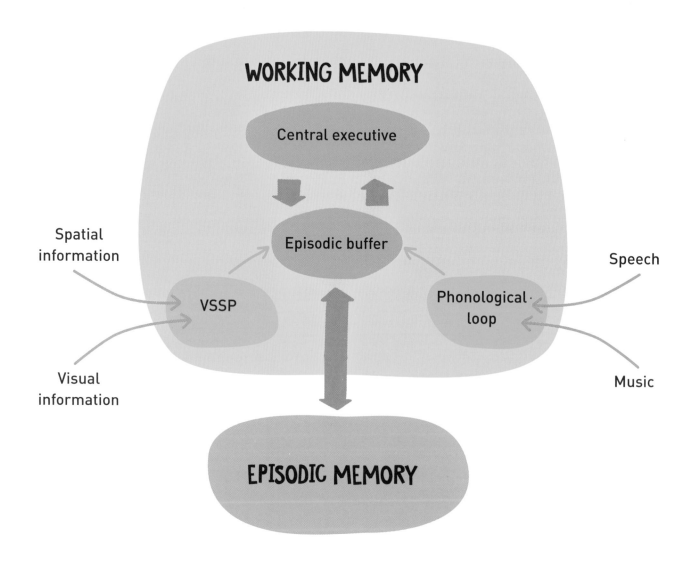

THINKING ABOUT COGNITIVE PSYCHOLOGY

In this chapter, we have used the topic of memory to explore some of the key concepts and assumptions of contemporary cognitive psychology. We have seen how Ebbinghaus developed methods to objectively measure recall. Sir Frederick Bartlett rejected these methods and focused on remembering as a constructive process.

In the 1950s and 1960s concepts from cybernetics and information theory gave psychologists a way of understanding the mind in terms of information processing that promised to be objective and precise. Donald Broadbent in 1958 put forward an information processing model that conceptualised the mind as a set of channels, filters, stores, processors and effectors which proved highly influential. Atkinson and Shiffrin developed the Multi Modal theory of memory which Alan Baddeley further developed.

Evidence for the existence of different memory stores was obtained from experimental studies of recall but also from case studies of individuals who through disease or surgery had developed very particular memory deficits. Memory research is still a very active area of research in cognitive psychology and the use of new brain imaging techniques is promising to add another dimension to our future understanding of the area. Note that memory is just one aspect of cognitive psychology. Other equally important areas of cognitive psychology include the study of perception, language and problem solving.

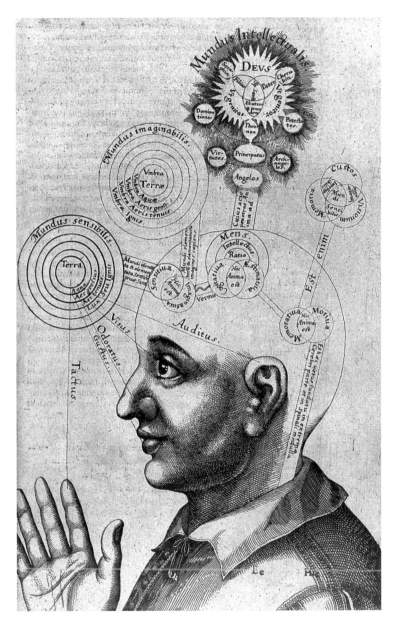

Cognitive psychology has sought to understand how memory works, from Ebbinghaus' early experiments on recall to Broadbent's theories on information processing and Baddeley's Working Memory Model.

COGNITIVE PSYCHOLOGY

Aristotle distinguished between material causes (substance), formal causes (design), efficient causes (what brings about change) and final causes (the goal or purpose). As humans, we can think and reflect and might, for example, design a university (formal cause) that is built from concrete (material cause) and is kept going by lecturers, students, administrators and house staff (efficient causes) in order to produce knowledge (final cause). Central to his account is the idea of purpose and the setting of goals. When Descartes split mind and body, purpose was an activity of the 'soul'. For materialistically minded psychologists, who rejected the notion of 'soul', the question of how our ability to think, reflect and plan could be accommodated into the natural world was a major problem.

The behaviourist solution was to banish the very concept of mind – and with it cognition – from psychology. The study of thinking was kept alive by gestalt psychologists such as Max Wertheimer, who published *Productive Thinking* (1945), and the developmental psychologist Jean Piaget (1896–1980), who published *The Psychology of Intelligence* (1947, original French edition).

In the 1940s and 1950s, cyberneticists, such as Norbert Wiener (1894–1964), and information theorists, such as Claude Shannon (1916–2001), gave psychologists a way of addressing how goal-directed behaviour could be addressed without bringing back the 'soul'. In 1956, a conference was held at Dartmouth College to explore the conjecture that language, problem-solving and all aspects of human intelligence could be simulated by machines. George A. Miller (1920–2012) and his colleagues published *Plans and the Structure of Behaviour* (1960), which further opened up the study of cognition as a respectable scientific pursuit. Ulric Neisser (1928–2012) published *Cognitive Psychology* (1967), which inspired a whole generation of psychologists to switch from the study of behaviour to the study of cognition.

A conference was held in Dartmouth College, New Hampshire, in 1956 to ask whether machines could simulate all aspects of human intelligence.

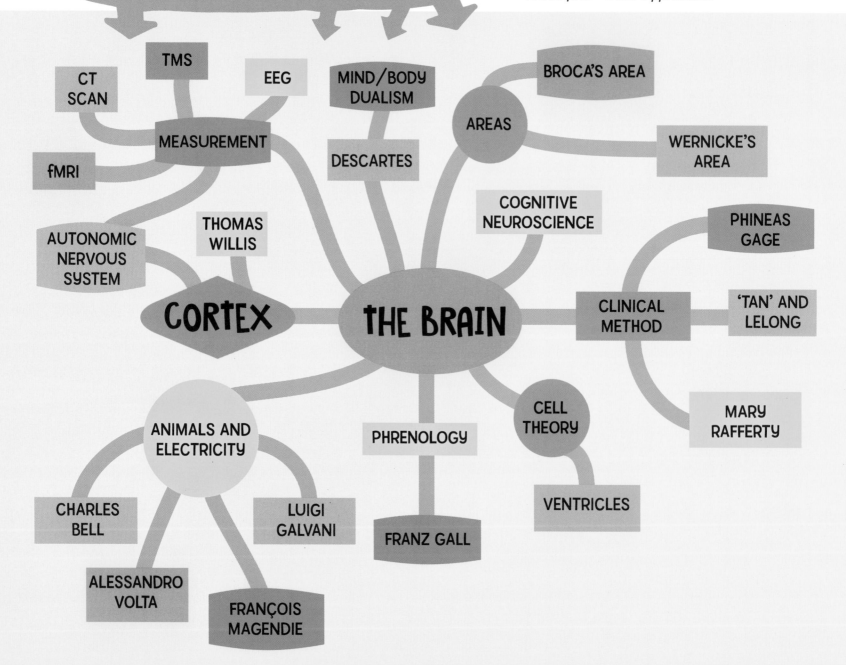

Chapter Four
BIOLOGICAL PSYCHOLOGY

Brain and Nervous System – Early Ideas – Cerebrum and Cortex – Localisation of Brain Function – Faculties and Phrenology – Nerve Impulses – Electrical Activity of Cortex – Ablation and Clinical Method – Non-invasive Techniques – Other Approaches

TMS

CT SCAN

EEG

MIND/BODY DUALISM

BROCA'S AREA

AREAS

WERNICKE'S AREA

MEASUREMENT

fMRI

DESCARTES

COGNITIVE NEUROSCIENCE

PHINEAS GAGE

AUTONOMIC NERVOUS SYSTEM

THOMAS WILLIS

CORTEX

THE BRAIN

CLINICAL METHOD

'TAN' AND LELONG

ANIMALS AND ELECTRICITY

PHRENOLOGY

CELL THEORY

MARY RAFFERTY

CHARLES BELL

LUIGI GALVANI

VENTRICLES

ALESSANDRO VOLTA

FRANZ GALL

FRANÇOIS MAGENDIE

BRAIN AND NERVOUS SYSTEM

For the learning theorists we met in Chapter 2, the working of the brain and nervous system is very interesting and definitely worthy of study in its own right, but it is a branch of *physiology* – not psychology proper. Some psychologists believe that theories in psychology can be studied without reference to the brain and nervous system, just as, say, it is possible to study art without a thorough understanding of chemistry. It might be useful to know about the chemistry of artists' paint but not essential to understand art. However, for most psychologists, some knowledge of the brain and nervous system is useful, given the intimate connection between mind and brain that we now take for granted.

Physiology for psychologists

COGNITIVE NEUROSCIENCE ▶ *combines research on the anatomy of the brain with experimental psychology.*

Cognitive neuroscientists believe that it is essential to understand the brain and nervous system and argue that a fully developed *cognitive neuroscience* will integrate research from experimental psychology with research on brain anatomy and the organisation of the nervous system to give us a complete picture of human psychology. In this chapter we review how our understanding of the brain and nervous system has developed over the last thousand or so years and describe some of the new and powerful techniques that are allowing us to understand more clearly the relationship between mind and brain.

Cognitive neuroscience

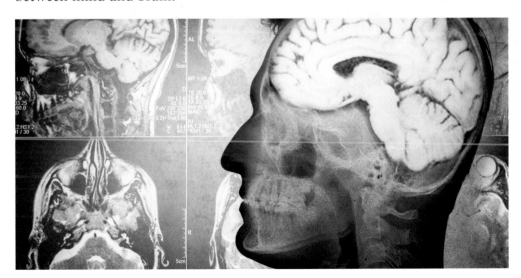

Cognitive neuroscientists believe that we must first understand the brain's anatomy and the nervous system before we can understand human psychology.

Gustav Fechner used himself as a test subject to learn more about perceptual judgements.

Gustav Fechner (1801–1887) is known as the father of **psychophysics** (the investigation of the relationship between physical stimuli and our psychological judgements of those physical stimuli). In a series of experiments using himself as a participant, he tested his own ability to discriminate between different weights. He found that his power to distinguish between them depended not on their absolute weight but on their relative weight to each other. This, he argued, was true of all stimuli. For example, if one were in a dark room, a single candle would dramatically increase the illumination in the room. The addition of a second candle would produce a noticeable difference. As more candles were lit we would notice less of a change. If there were 100 candles lighting up the room, the addition of the 101st would make very little difference to us.

The ancient Greeks believed that what gave humans life and the ability to think was the flow of a mysterious substance called **pneuma** that permeated our bodies and the universe. This mysterious substance might be likened to an animating 'breath of life' that is with us while we live and disappears when we die. How this pneuma circulated around the human body was open to debate. But the prevailing view was that it travelled around the body via 'pores' or 'channels'. They called these pores **'nerves'**.

For Plato, the circulation of pneuma through the brain gave rise to rational thought.

For Aristotle, the heart was the site of human rationality and the brain was simply a kind of cooling system that sat on top of our heads!

The importance of these nerves was demonstrated by the physician and surgeon Galen who, in a famous and appalling experiment, quietened the squeals of a dying pig by tying a thread around the vagus nerve and gradually tightening it. Its squeals could be brought back by slackening the thread and 'allowing the flow of pneuma to return'. In experiments like this, Galen was able to demonstrate that the nerves formed a system connecting different parts of the body. He believed that the circulation of pneuma was crucial to mental activity. So, after dissecting various mammals, he came to the conclusion that it was the hollow chambers or **ventricles** he found in the middle of their brains that were the site of all mental activity, and not the brain tissue itself.

This view dominated medical and anatomical thinking for the next 1,500 years as first Greek, then Roman and finally Arab scientists elaborated on what became known as the **cell theory** of brain function. They believed that the connected ventricles of the brain were responsible for different mental functions or **faculties**, such as sensation, imagination, memory, practical reason and creative reason.

> ## CELL THEORY OF THE BRAIN ▶ *each ventricle of the brain is responsible for a different mental function.*

THE IMPORTANCE OF THE CEREBRUM AND CORTEX

Site of cognition

It was not until the seventeenth century that realisation began to dawn that the ventricles were not the active site of the brain. In fact, it was the, at first glance, rather dull and inert outer 'bark' or cortex of the brain that was the location of learning and cognition. While carrying out post mortems to determine cause of death, Thomas Willis (1621–75) took the opportunity to very carefully dissect the brains of his subjects. He was assisted by his colleague Christopher Wren (later to be knighted for his architectural work). Willis worked in very difficult conditions. There were no electric lights or refrigeration, and brain tissue, when fresh, has been described as having the consistency of soft curd cheese. Yet he produced a precise and accurate anatomy of the brain.

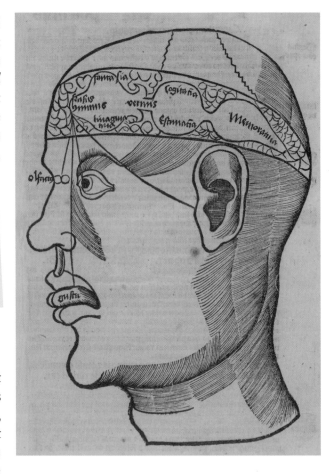

A medieval illustration of the cell theory of the organization of mental faculties.

Willis still understood the functioning of the brain in terms of the movement of pneuma but his anatomical investigations moved the focus from the ventricles on the inside of the brain to the outer cortex as the site of mental faculties. The problem now was to localise these faculties in the brain tissue itself.

Sir Christopher Wren and Thomas Willis carefully dissected the brains of their subjects, greatly enhancing our knowledge of the brain's anatomy.

LOCALISATION OF BRAIN FUNCTION

Proponents of the cell theory and later anatomists such as Willis understood the mind as a collection of faculties. René Descartes moved the debate on by developing an understanding of the relationship between mind and body.

The response of the British empiricists to Descartes' rationalism was to argue that the contents of the mental realm (ideas and images) were the less vivid impressions left by our sensations of the world around us. All that is in our minds originated in our experiences, and from this philosophical principle rather than empirical studies of the brain or studies of actual learning argued that complex human cognition must be the result of the forging of associations between sensations and ideas.

Philosophical principles

René Descartes and Cartesian Mind Body dualism

René Descartes (1596–1650) attempted to reform philosophy by searching for a starting point which was absolutely certain. Using a method of radical doubt, he rejected the authority of experts and his own senses ending up only being certain of his activity of doubting. This indubitable activity was a kind of thinking hence his famous statement cogito ergo sum – I think therefore I am. This solution resulted in a fundamental split between mind and matter also mind and body. He proposed that the mind could control the body through the pineal gland which lies at the very centre of the brain. The pineal gland, he argued was affected by changes in the flow of pneuma caused by stimulation of the nerves. The soul could then use the pineal gland to direct pneuma back down the nerves to produce movement. The body according to Descartes was simply a machine directed by the mind which was an aspect of the non-physical soul.

This *associationist* account of the mind proved amenable to the *behaviourist* theories of learning we examined in Chapter 2. The empiricists' reluctance to speculate on the brain was in many ways very sensible because there was no empirical way of establishing links between brain and behaviour. This set in opposition those who believed that the brain was made up of separate faculties and those who viewed the brain as a more general-purpose organ. In the 18th century, the faculty psychologists gained a new following when Franz Gall (1758–1828) began researching the connection between brain, behaviour and the shape of the skull.

NAMES TO KNOW: ANATOMISTS OF THE BRAIN

Thomas Willis (1621–75)

Sir Christopher Wren (1632–1723)

Franz Gall Gall (1758–1828)

Franz Gall discovered the contralateral function – that the right side of the brain controls the left side of the body, and the left of the brain controls the right side of the body.

FACULTIES AND PHRENOLOGY

Gall was clear that the brain was the specific organ of mental activity and conducted some precise and careful anatomical work on neuroanatomy. He was one of the first researchers to confirm from examining the brain what we now know as its *contralateral function* – that is, that the right side of the brain controls the left side of the body and vice versa. Recognising that he couldn't study the living brain directly, Gall reasoned that it was necessary to find indirect means to study the brain's faculties.

Contralateral function

71

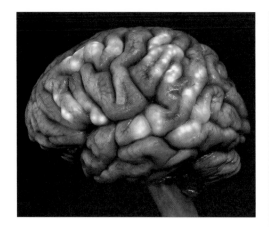

The living brain is soft. It is only after hardening that it is easy to dissect.

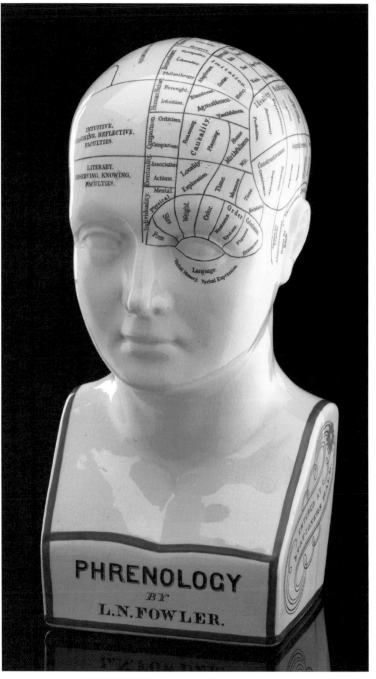

Gall's phrenology sparked an interest in where in the brain different mental functions were carried out.

His starting point was that, just as looking at mountains, valleys and rivers provides us with information about the underlying geology, examining the bumps and hollows of the skull would tell us about the underlying development of the brain. Faculties that were particularly well developed would be bigger and this would give rise to bigger bumps. This turned out to be a very serious error. The thickness of the skull is not related in a systematic way to underlying brain functioning except in very rare cases of brain disease. Nevertheless, Gall's *phrenology* became very popular and people paid to have their skulls examined by Gall and his colleagues. Gall collected the skulls of eminent people and criminals and produced complex 'atlases' showing the geography of the faculties in terms of the bumps and hollows of the skull.

ANIMAL ELECTRICITY AND THE NERVOUS IMPULSE

From Willis to Gall, great attention was paid to the structure of the brain. In the eighteenth century, a breakthrough was made in understanding brain activity when Luigi Galvani (1737 –98) discovered that the nerve impulse could be started electrically; he had observed that the leg of a dead frog twitched violently when touched by a metal knife. Galvani hypothesised that the muscles of the frog must contain 'animal electricity' that was released by the metal knife. This may seem an odd conclusion. But in Galvani's time it was already known that some species of eel could give one a nasty shock. So it seemed that electricity was something that was found inside an organism and could be released in this way. Alessandro Volta (1745–1827), however, showed that it wasn't internal animal electricity that caused the frog's leg to twitch but static electricity charging the knife and stimulating the frog's muscle.

Galvani and Volta

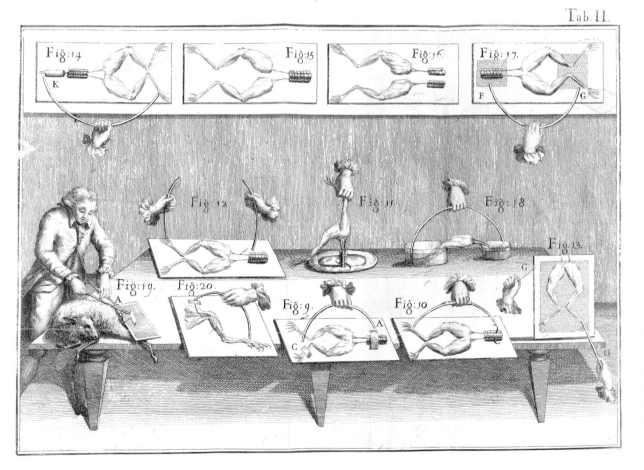

Luigi Galvani believed that the muscles must carry 'animal electricity' to explain why the frog legs twitched when touched by a metal knife.

Sir Charles Bell pioneered research of the structure of the nervous system.

The frog rapidly became the organism of choice for studying the relationship between nerves and muscles. Volta discovered that the muscle twitch could be produced even when the frog was decapitated, thus showing that *reflex* action occurs without intervention from the brain.

This laid the ground for further exploration of the structure of the nervous system and, working independently, Sir Charles Bell (1774–1842) in England and François Magendie (1783–1855) in France argued that the nervous system was organised in terms of sensory (*afferent*) and motor (*efferent*) nerves.

NAMES TO KNOW: NEUROANATOMISTS

Luigi Galvani (1737–98)

Alessandro Volta (1745–1827)

Sir Charles Bell (1774–1842)

François Magendie (1783–1855)

Bell discovered the distinction through observation and anatomical dissection. Magendie discovered this through experiments on live animals (puppies!) in which he systematically cut the nerves to show how movement and sensitivity were governed by different nerve pathways. Bell and Magendie and their followers disputed who had come up with the observation first. Now both scientists are honoured as discoverers of the so-called Bell–Magendie Law.

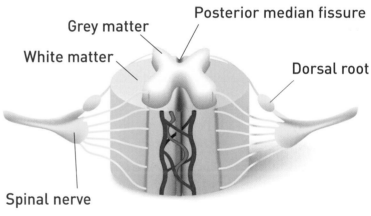

How the afferent and efferent nerves enter the spinal column.

François Magendie argued that the nervous system was organised into afferent and efferent nerves.

ELECTRICAL ACTIVITY OF THE CORTEX

The Autonomic and Sympathetic Nervous Systems

These early researchers discovered that the nervous system was divided between movement that could be produced at will (such as that of the respirator muscles) and involuntary movement that could not be controlled at will (such as those of the heart and intestines). Others made a distinction between what they called the 'animal nervous system' and the 'vegetative nervous system'. John Newport Langley introduced the terms *autonomic* and *sympathetic* nervous systems to cover these distinctions, which are still used today.

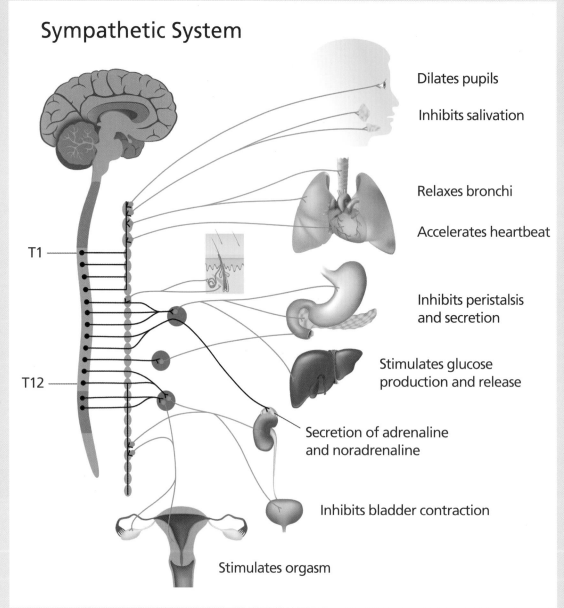

Sympathetic System

Dilates pupils

Inhibits salivation

Relaxes bronchi

Accelerates heartbeat

Inhibits peristalsis and secretion

Stimulates glucose production and release

Secretion of adrenaline and noradrenaline

Inhibits bladder contraction

Stimulates orgasm

T1

T12

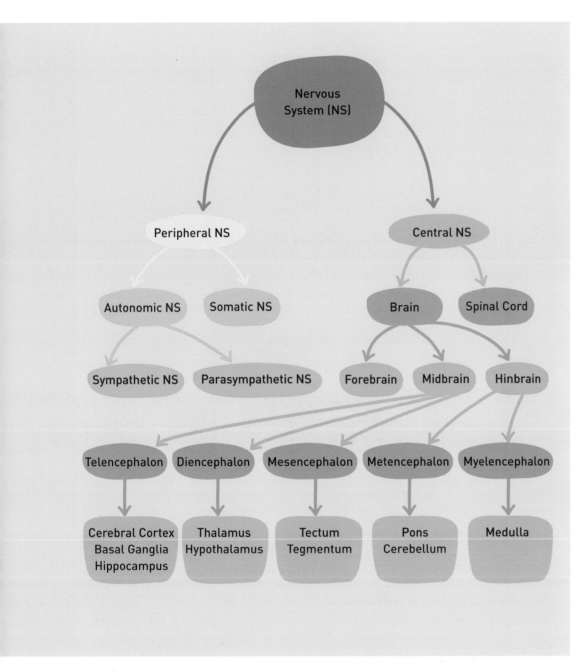

NAMES TO KNOW:
UNDERSTANDING THE CORTEX

Eduard Hitzig (1838–1907)

Gustav Fritsch (1838–1927)

David Ferrier (1843–1928)

While it was relatively straightforward to demonstrate how reflex actions could be stimulated by applying an electric current, the activity of the cortex was very much a mystery. It was not until the end of the nineteenth century that Eduard Hitzig and Gustav Fritsch demonstrated the electrical activity of the brain itself.

Eduard Hitzig and Gustav Fritsch established that the brain itself had substantial electrical activity.

In 1870, they achieved this by exposing the cerebral cortex of a dog and stimulating different regions with electrodes. They discovered a strip across the frontal cortex that was associated with the execution of movement. This area is now known as the *motor cortex*. This research was extended by David Ferrier (1843–1928) who, experimenting on monkeys, identified separate *sensory* and *motor* regions of the cortex. He also found that the area of the brain given over to a function was proportional to the sensitivity of the function. For example, a large area of the sensory cortex is given over to the functions of the lips and tongue as these areas are very sensitive. Far less is given over to the back, even though it occupies a much larger area of the body, because it is far less sensitive. His experiments, just as those conducted by Magendie before him, caused an outcry in the UK and led to him being prosecuted for animal cruelty.

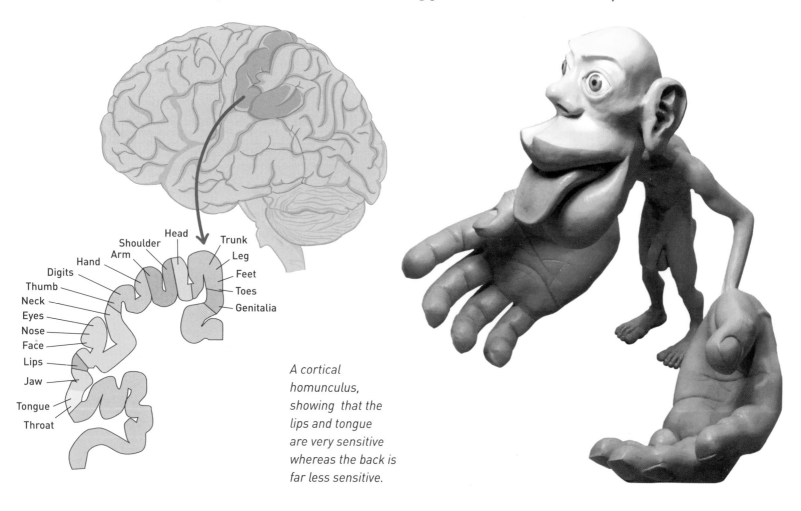

A cortical homunculus, showing that the lips and tongue are very sensitive whereas the back is far less sensitive.

ABLATION AND CLINICAL METHOD

Great strides were made in understanding the anatomy of the nervous system but one of the big problems was that, for ethical reasons, studies were limited to frogs and other animals or human cadavers. What was needed was a way of studying the living and linking mental functioning with the underlying nervous system. One way in which this was achieved was by studying individuals whose brain has been damaged and carefully observing how their behaviour differed from the normal population. This is the clinical method and was, perhaps, most famously employed by Dr Pierre Paul Broca (1824–80). As head of a psychiatric hospital, Broca treated a patient known as 'Tan' (Louis Victor Leborgne) who, at 51 years of age, could only repeat the words 'tan-tan' and a few swear words. He had been in this state for 21 years. When 'Tan' died, Broca carried out a post-mortem examination and discovered a damaged area in a part of 'Tan's' brain.

Studying brain damage

Dr Paul Broca carried out a post-mortem examination of his patient Tan's brain to discover the causes of his mental illness.

Carl Wernicke discovered the area of the brain responsible for speech.

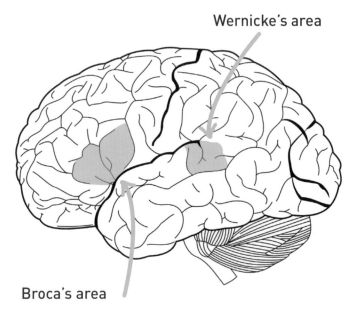

Wernicke's area

Broca's area

Broca later carried out a post-mortem on a second patient known as Lazare Lelong who was being treated for dementia. This 84-year-old could only say five words: 'oui', 'non', 'tois' [trois], 'toujours' and 'Lelo' (an attempt to say his own name). When Broca carried out a post-mortem examination on Lelong, he discovered damage that largely corresponded to the same area of the brain as in 'Tan'. This was important because it linked a particular ability (speech production) with a very specific area of the brain. The condition they both suffered was later called Broca's *aphasia* and the part of the brain involved is known as Broca's area.

In Germany, Carl Wernicke (1848–1905) examined patients who had different speech problems from those of 'Tan' and Lelong. These patients had no problem producing speech but could not string together meaningful sentences. When he examined their brains post-mortem he found a different but nearby area of the brain had been damaged. These clinical cases were very informative and provided evidence for localisation of brain function but they were problematic because the evidence was observational only. Another source of evidence for location of function came from traumatic brain injury. The story of Phineas Gage, who experienced a terribly violent trauma, became one of the most famous cases in the history of neurology.

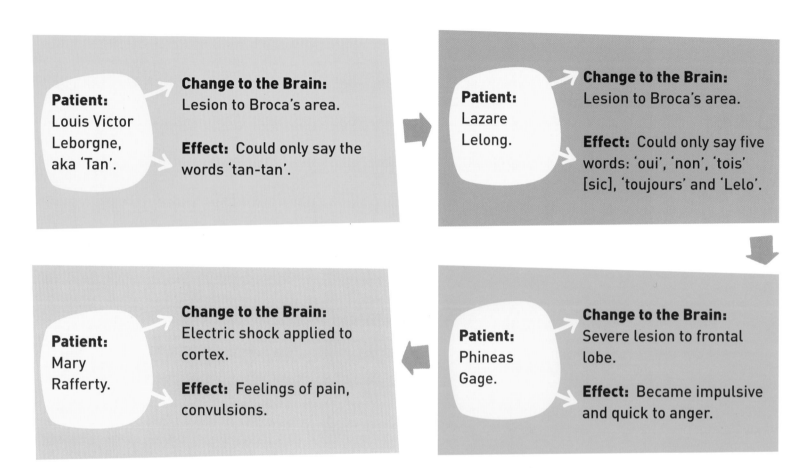

Patient: Louis Victor Leborgne, aka 'Tan'.

Change to the Brain: Lesion to Broca's area.

Effect: Could only say the words 'tan-tan'.

Patient: Lazare Lelong.

Change to the Brain: Lesion to Broca's area.

Effect: Could only say five words: 'oui', 'non', 'tois' [sic], 'toujours' and 'Lelo'.

Patient: Mary Rafferty.

Change to the Brain: Electric shock applied to cortex.

Effect: Feelings of pain, convulsions.

Patient: Phineas Gage.

Change to the Brain: Severe lesion to frontal lobe.

Effect: Became impulsive and quick to anger.

Phineas Gage (1823–60)

Gage was working on the construction of a railroad in the USA. His job involved drilling holes in rock, filling the holes with dynamite, and then packing the explosive in tightly using a metal rod or 'tamping iron'. On one occasion the dynamite exploded and the metal rod was blasted through the front of Gage's head. Miraculously, he survived this accident. Gage's case was remarkable, not only because he survived the catastrophic damage to his brain but because his doctor, John Harlow, *John Harlow* wrote up the case history and followed Gage's subsequent progress. According to Harlow, what was apparent was that Gage's temperament was noticeably different after the accident. Before the accident he had been, according to reports, easy going and affable. Afterwards he was impulsive and quick to anger. Harlow, a phrenologist, cited this as evidence for the localisation of mental faculties, suggesting that the accident had disturbed the basic brain organisation.

NAMES TO KNOW:
EXPERIMENTING ON THE BRAIN

Marie Jean Pierre Flourens
(1794–1867)

Paul Broca *(1824–80)*

Roberts Bartholow *(1831–1904)*

Carl Wernicke *(1848–1905)*

Hans Berger *(1873 – 1941)*

The skull of Phineas Gage shows the substantial damage he received to his brain, which noticeably changed his personality.

Marie Jean Pierre Flourens

Case studies of diseased brains and brain accidents could not by themselves provide conclusive proof of the brain–localisation hypothesis. The case of Phineas Gage is suggestive but the brain damage he suffered was the result of a brutal accident that would likely have changed him anyway. The region of the brain damaged was quite widespread and so not precise enough to localise a particular function. The areas identified by Broca and Wernicke were precise but relied on finding individuals who suffered very specific diseases. These methods were *observational*. They did not involve experimentation to demonstrate how changes in the brain caused changes in cognitive functioning.

Marie Jean Pierre Flourens (1794–1867) was an avowed experimentalist and critic of the faculty hypothesis. He carried out experiments on animals, usually rabbits and pigeons, in which he selectively and systematically

EXTRAORDINARY ACCIDENT AND CURE

WE FIND THE FOLLOWING account of an extraordinary cure in the *Union Medicale*: Phineas Gage, aged 25, employed in the construction of a railway, was engaged in charging a hole made in a rock with powder in order to blast it, when, supposing that the powder had become mixed with sand, he stirred it up with a long iron rod. An explosion instantly took place, and the bar was driven completely through the head of the man and fell at a short distance from him, covered with blood and a part of his brain. The iron rod weighed about 6lb., was 34 inches in length, and about an inch thick. It entered the left angle of the lower jaw, and came out at the top of the head behind the bone of the forehead. The wounded man was knocked down by the blow, but immediately rose again, spoke to the persons round him, got up into a cart, in which he kept standing while it was being driven for more than a mile to an inn, where he alighted and ascended a long staircase, and went to bed in the possession of his mental faculties. A surgeon arrived in half an hour after the accident. The upper part of the head was extensively fractured and the wound at the side of the jaw was large enough to admit the finger. The small pieces of the skull were removed, the larger bones adjusted, and the wounds dressed. We shall not enter into the details of this interesting case, but merely say that the patient promptly recovered with the loss only of the sight of the left eye.

The Times, Friday, 6 December 1850

removed brain tissue and observed the behavioural effects. He found that removing the cerebral hemispheres abolished all perceptions, motoricity and judgement and so he concluded that they were responsible for higher cognitive functions. Removal of the cerebellum abolished the animal's equilibrium and motor co-ordination and was therefore presumed responsible for regulating and integrating movement. Removing the brain stem (***medulla oblongata***) caused death. Magendie found no evidence that specific regions of the brain were responsible for memory and cognition.

Medulla oblongata

The big problem he faced was how to study the living brain and especially the cortex. In 1874, Roberts Bartholow (1831–1904) carried out tests on one of his patients, Mary Rafferty, who had lost part of her skull as a result of cancer. This had left the top of her brain exposed. Using a probe, Bartholow applied a small electric current to her cortex. As he increased the current she reported feelings of pain and went into convulsions. She died a few days later. Bartholow's experiment was, by the standards of today, completely unethical because he inflicted pain and may have hastened Mary's death simply to satisfy his curiosity. Nevertheless, he has been recorded in the history books as the first person to demonstrate the electrical excitability of the human cortex.

The Lobes of the Brain

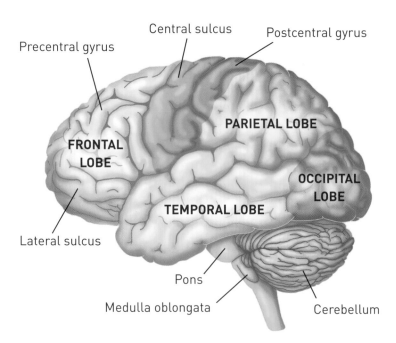

Precentral gyrus

Central sulcus

Postcentral gyrus

PARIETAL LOBE

FRONTAL LOBE

OCCIPITAL LOBE

TEMPORAL LOBE

Lateral sulcus

Pons

Medulla oblongata

Cerebellum

Anatomists divide the two sides of the brain into four different areas or lobes: the frontal, parietal, occipital and temporal lobes. Each area is associated with a different set of cognitive functions.

EEG AND THE DEVELOPMENT OF NON-INVASIVE APPROACHES

We now know that Gall was wrong about the thickness of the skull being an indicator of underlying brain function. But it has turned out that the skull is not an impenetrable barrier to understanding brain function. Gall's assumptions may have been wrong headed but the ambition to measure brain activity has remained very strong. Hans Berger (1873–1941) first attempted to measure the activity of the human brain by measuring changes in the pressure of blood flow through exposed regions of the cortex of patients who had suffered brain injuries. He reasoned that increased blood flow indicated increased activity. This approach was not successful so he tried measuring the electrical activity of the brain by placing electrodes into the tissue covering the skull. By refining his technique, he was able to place electrodes on the surface of the skull to measure electrical activity. He then began using amplifiers and was able to record the small changes in electrical activity caused by nerve impulses in the outer cortex of the brain, without the need for surgical intervention. These were the first measurements of *electroencephalography* (EEG).

ELECTROENCEPHALOGRAPHY ▶ *the measurement of brain activity through the electrical signals it produces.*

He found that when recordings were made with the eyes closed and in a relaxed state the waves were of relatively low frequency. When the eyes were open and engaged in mental activity the frequency increased. The *brain waves* at rest are known as *alpha waves*; those produced when alert are known as beta waves. Since Berger's early work, other waves have been discovered. *Theta waves* are produced when dropping off to sleep and *delta waves* occur during deep sleep.

Twenty-first-Century Functional Brain Imaging

So far we have considered how ideas about the structure and function of the nervous system developed from ancient Greece to the early years of the twentieth century. Arguments about whether mental functions were localised or spread through the brain raged for over 100 years. The techniques used to study the brain and nervous system became more sophisticated, moving from the autopsy table to measuring the electrical activity of the whole brain. Towards the end of the twentieth century and into the twenty-first century, techniques used to study the active, living brain have become even more sophisticated. Although Berger abandoned the direct study of blood flow through the brain and invented EEG, new methods have allowed researchers to measure changes in blood flow, as well as oxygen consumption and glucose utilisation, that indicate changes in mental activity. These methods allow activity in the living brain to be observed. *Transcranial magnetic stimulation* (TMS), developed in the 1980s, offers the promise of stimulating the brain without using dangerous or invasive techniques and moving beyond observational studies.

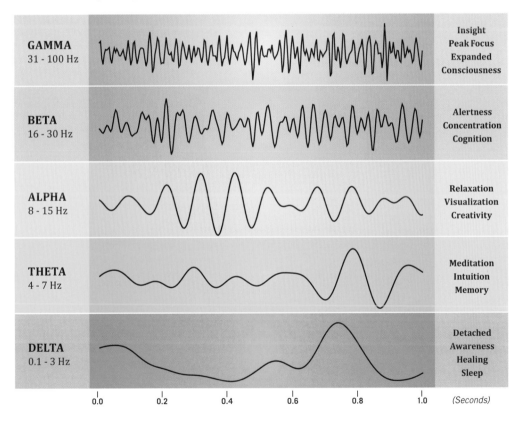

Different brain waves and their relative frequencies.

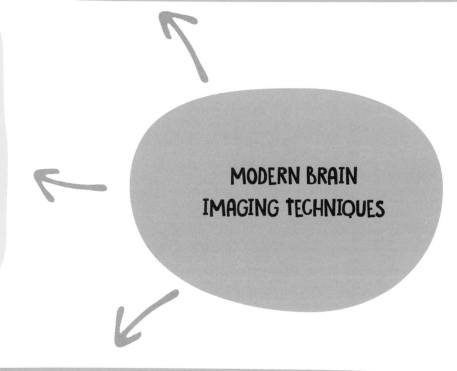

MAGNETOCEPHALOGRAPHY (MEG)
measures the magnetic activity of the brain. It measures the same activity as EEG but has better spatial resolution (>10 mm). MEG requires the participant to be placed in a magnetically shielded room with their head placed inside the MEG machine.

ELECTROENCEPHALOGRAPHY (EEG)
measures the electrical activity of the brain. It is used to capture the firing of networks of neurons and has high temporal resolution so that the effects of presenting a stimulus to an experimental participant can be measured less than 1 millisecond afterwards. Spatial resolution is low so cannot distinguish between areas firing below 10mm.

MODERN BRAIN IMAGING TECHNIQUES

POSITRON EMISSION TOMOGRAPHY (PET)
measures concentrations of chemicals such as water, glucose and neurotransmitters to identify neurochemical pathways. The temporal resolution is low (10 seconds +). The technique requires participants to ingest small doses of radioactive material which has meant that it has been superceded by functional Magnetic Resonance Imaging (fMRI).

fMRI

measures the Blood Oxygen Level (BOLD) signal to distinguish between active and inactive regions of the brain. Has excellent spatial resolution <5mm but relatively slow temporal resolution (200 milliseconds +).

TRANSCRANIAL MAGNETIC STIMULATION (TMS)

is a non-invasive technique to produce pain free and reversible lesions in the brain. The technique uses a strong magnet to disrupt the activity of networks of neurons. Spatial resolution is between 5–10 mm and temporal resolution is less than half a second.

SUMMARY

The chapter has focused on the historical development of our understanding of the brain and nervous system from a pneumatic conception of hollow pipes transmitting fluids and 'pneuma' around the body to a mechanistic model of reflexes to today's understanding of the nervous system as an electrochemical system. Along the way, neuroscientists and anatomists argued about how the brain functioned, debating whether or not the brain was a relatively undifferentiated organ which needed to be investigated as a functional whole, or if it were better understood as a collection of very specific functions that could be mapped to precise areas of the cortex. Psychologists and neuroscientists now have access to methods and techniques to study the functioning of the active brain that were unheard of less than thirty years ago. These methods and techniques are still being developed and promise to deepen our understanding of the relationship between mind and brain.

BIOLOGICAL PSYCHOLOGY

The development of biological psychology is closely linked to allied disciplines including medicine, neurophysiology and *psychiatry*. The Greek physician and surgeon Galen (129–c.216), who practised during the Roman Empire, identified thinking and reasoning with the circulation of psychic pneuma through the ventricles of the brain and then on to the rest of the body via neurons. Variations on the ventricular theory multiplied over the next thousand years, but Galen's basic blueprint of the organisation of the nervous system went unchallenged. Andreas Vesalius (1514–64), a Belgian anatomist who was, unlike Galen, permitted to carry out dissections of people, questioned Galen's observations and stimulated new interest in anatomy.

Through the seventeenth and eighteenth centuries, the anatomical structures of the nervous system were thoroughly explored and more sophisticated and accurate maps of the brain were widely disseminated, such as Thomas Willis's (1621–75) *Cerebri Anatome* (1664).

In the nineteenth century, clinicians such as Paul Broca (1824–80) and Carl Wernicke (1848–1905) were able to precisely identify areas of the brain with particular psychological functions. The discovery of the electrical and chemical mechanisms of nerve transmission gave us a new understanding of how the nervous system was integrated. The use of electrical stimulation of the brain by David Ferrier (1843–1928) allowed the systematic investigation of the relationship between behaviour and anatomy to be explored. During the first half of the 20th century, methods such as *EEG*, invented by Hans Berger (1873–1941), allowed the first non-invasive studies of brain function to be carried out. In the last quarter of the twentieth century, the development of non-invasive techniques such as *fMRI*, discovered by Seiji Ogawa (1934–present), and transcranial magnetic stimulation (TMS), by Anthony Barker (1950–present), have dramatically increased our knowledge of the brain and nervous system.

Andreas Vesalius questioned Galen's assumptions and stimulated new interest in human anatomy.

Chapter Five
DEVELOPMENTAL PSYCHOLOGY

Nurture and Education – Genetic Epistemology – Piaget's Stage Theory – Social Constructionist Approaches – Psychoanalytic Approach – Attachment Theory – Moral Development – Other Approaches

EVOLUTIONARY APPROACH

PHYLOGENETIC

ANTHROPOLOGICAL

PSYCHOANALYTIC

ROUSSEAU

CHILDREN AS SINFUL

DARWIN

STRUCTURE AND SCHEMAS

JEAN PIAGET

STAGE THEORY

PHILOSOPHICAL APPROACH

JAMES MARK BALDWIN

GENETIC EPISTEMOLOGY

ASSIMILATION AND ACCOMMODATIONS

ENCULTURATION

EDUCATION AND CHILDREN

DEVELOPMENTAL PSYCHOLOGY

SOCIAL CONSTRUCTIONISM

LEV VYGOTSKY

SOCIAL LEARNING THEORY

ALBERT BANDURA

JEROME BRUNER

SIGMUND FREUD

ATTACHMENT THEORY

ZONE OF PROXIMAL DEVELOPMENT

SPIRAL CURRICULUM

OEDIPUS COMPLEX

SCAFFOLDING

PSYCHOANALYSIS

STRANGE SITUATION TEST

JOHN BOWLBY

MORAL DEVELOPMENT

KOHLBERG'S STAGES

NURTURE AND EDUCATION

The nurture and education of children, healthy in mind and body, to take their place in adult society has long been important to concerned parents and anxious teachers and philosophers alike. The philosopher Jean-Jacques Rousseau (1712–78) was a stern critic of the way his own society raised and taught its children. In 1762, he wrote an account of the education of two fictional children, Émile and Sophie, in order to draw attention to the prevailing attitudes of the time. This was a period when, essentially, children were regarded as sinful beings who needed to have the badness beaten out of them and to have, at least for the upper classes, learning drilled into them. Rousseau's alternative concept was that children were basically good and needed to actively learn from experience in order to become independent citizens who were resilient enough to withstand living in a corrupt society.

Jean-Jacques Rousseau

Jean-Jacques Rousseau's views on the nature of children were hugely influential.

NAMES TO KNOW: EARLY PEDAGOGUES

Jean-Jacques Rousseau (1712–78)

Johann Heinrich Pestalozzi (1746–1827)

Friedrich Froebel (1782–1852)

Rousseau's views influenced at least two generations of teachers or *pedagogues*, including the Swiss educational reformer Johann Heinrich Pestalozzi (1746–1827). He described his own approach to education in his work *How Gertrude Teaches Her Children* (1894). Pestalozzi went on to found his own schools and led the programme to increase literacy in Switzerland. Friedrich Froebel (1782–1852) was another teacher who was hugely influenced by Rousseau. Froebel was instrumental in popularising *Kindergarten* as an institution in which very young children could learn through play and social interaction before moving on to more formal teaching.

These principles were further developed by Maria Montessori (1870–1952) who used her experiences of working with children with special educational needs to develop a set of general pedagogic principles. Children are taught in mixed age classes to encourage peer learning and instead of a fixed curriculum allowed to explore and learn at their own pace.

Friedrich Froebel helped spread the idea of the Kindergarten as a way to help children learn through play before they began their formal education.

Evolution

These educational initiatives were based on philosophical speculation along with the practical experience of the pedagogues who launched them. However, they were not based on systematic empirical research into how children developed or learned. The systematic approach to understanding children and how they change over time can be traced back to the naturalist Charles Darwin. Darwin was keen to demonstrate that human behaviour was cut from the same cloth as animal behaviour. To further his research, he kept extensive notes, not just about the natural world around him, but also of the behaviour of his own children.

Darwin and child behaviour

Charles Darwin's notes on child development formed the basis of the scientific study of developmental psychology.

Linking physical and mental

Darwin's notes, written in the 1840s, were not published until 1877 when 'A Biographical Sketch of an infant' appeared in the journal *Mind*. Darwin catalogued the capacities of one of his newborn or neonate children. He observed that the **neonate** demonstrated reflex behaviours including '*sneezing, hickuping, yawning, stretching, and of course sucking and screaming*'. He observed how the infant's awareness of the world progressed and expanded over time. For example, at about 49 days old, the baby was first observed fixating his gaze on an object. Darwin used these observations in his book *The Expression of the Emotions in Man and Animals* (1872) but he didn't develop a thorough-going psychology from his findings.

James Mark Baldwin (1861–1934) took up the evolutionary approach to understanding children. He argued that to get a full picture of what it is to be human it is necessary to consider development from three different perspectives. Baldwin attempted to correlate physical development with mental development and he investigated, among other things, handedness, colour perception and speech.

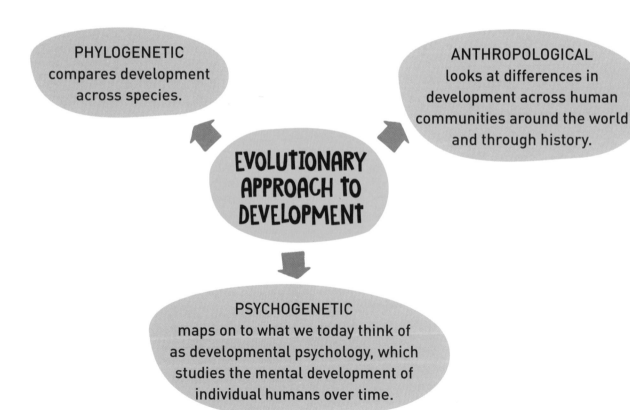

PHYLOGENETIC
compares development
across species.

ANTHROPOLOGICAL
looks at differences in
development across human
communities around the world
and through history.

EVOLUTIONARY
APPROACH TO
DEVELOPMENT

PSYCHOGENETIC
maps on to what we today think of
as developmental psychology, which
studies the mental development of
individual humans over time.

GENETIC EPISTEMOLOGY

Baldwin's attempt to synthesise biology and the growth of knowledge was also the ambition of Jean Piaget (1896–1980). Piaget was fascinated by the phenomenon of growth and the processes that lead to the formation of increasingly complex mental structures. He came to child development after spending time working with Alfred Binet (see Chapter 7) on standardised tests of intelligence. As Piaget administered tests to children of different ages, he came to realise that children of a similar age tended to make similar kinds of mistakes. By asking these children to explain their answers, Piaget believed that it was possible to identify the knowledge structures that underpinned the child's relation to the world.

Jean Piaget aimed to map human development from a newborn baby, capable of little more than a series of unconnected reflexes, to an adult capable of works of genius.

NAMES TO KNOW: BIOLOGY AND MENTAL DEVELOPMENT

Charles Darwin (1809–82)

James Mark Baldwin (1861–1934)

His goal then became to chart human development, starting with the neonate who was, as Darwin had observed, a crying bundle of unconnected reflexes. Piaget wanted to trace how these reflexes were integrated and developed until in adulthood a human has the capacity to produce works of scientific or artistic genius.

GENETIC EPISTEMOLOGY ▶ *the study of the growth of knowledge.*

Piaget called this undertaking *genetic epistemology;* 'genetic' because it is concerned with development and 'epistemology' because it is concerned with knowledge.

The key concept in Piaget's theory of development is *structure*. Contrary to the learning theorists described in Chapter 2, who believed that complex performance was the result of long chains of associations, Piaget believed that performance was the result of developing more and more complex, abstract and flexible models of the world. These models of the world, or *knowledge structures*, he called '*schemas*' and can be thought of as *organised patterns of thoughts and actions*.

Structures and schemas

NAMES TO KNOW: DEVELOPMENTAL PSYCHOLOGISTS

Jean Piaget *(1896–1980)*

Lev Vygotsky *(1896–1934)*

SCHEMAS ▶ *organized patterns of thoughts and actions or knowledge structures.*

PIAGET'S STAGE THEORY

According to Piaget, the knowledge structures, or *schemas*, that we use to understand the world do not grow gradually and cumulatively. Instead they proceed as a series of global qualitative shifts in overall structure, which he called 'stages' (compare the learning theorists' and Gestalt theorists' accounts of learning in Chapter 2). Evidence for the existence of these qualitatively different stages came from Piaget's study of his own children and later studies by his colleagues of larger groups of children.

Piaget's Experiments

Piaget argued that the ability to see a situation from another person's perspective was an important milestone in cognitive development and marked the shift from the **pre-operational stage** to the **concrete operational stage.** He investigated the development of 'changed perspectives' by devising a test called the 'Three Mountain Problem'.

For this problem, a child sits in front of a table on which have been placed three model mountains of different sizes. One mountain is covered in snow, one mountain is marked with a red cross at its summit and the other mountain has a hut on its top. The child is asked to have a good look at this mountain scene and walk round the table to see it from different angles. The experimenter now introduces a doll, which is placed at different positions around the mountain scene. The child is then asked to look at a selection of photographs taken of the mountains and indicate which one shows what the doll would see from its perspective.

Piaget found that younger children picked the scene they could see from their own vantage point, irrespective of where the doll was positioned. This indicated **egocentric** thought. At around the ages of seven or eight the child is able to identify the photograph that represents the doll's view of the mountain rather than the child's own.

A typical Piagetian experiment used to distinguish children at different stages of cognitive development.

Two processes drive the development of stages, *assimilation* and *accommodation*. A child is active in the world and experiences novel events and objects.

ASSIMILATION ▶ *describes how new experiences are incorporated into existing schemas.*

ACCOMMODATION ▶ *describes how some new experiences cannot be understood in terms of pre-existing schemas and the schema itself must change to adjust to these new circumstances.*

The progress of the child through these stages was invariant and universal. All children from all cultures pass through the same stages in the same order. On the surface, educational achievement might look very different across the world, but the underlying cognitive structures were the same.

AGE	STAGE	CHARACTERISTICS/ACHIEVEMENTS
Birth–2	Sensorimotor	Integration of the senses. Object permanence. Symbolic play.
2–6	Pre-operational	Egocentrism. Inability to conserve. Beginning of representational thought.
7–11	Concrete operational	Conservation in concrete situations. No longer egocentric.
12–adult	Formal operational	Logical thinking. Development of abstract thought.

The four stages of child mental development that Piaget identified and their characteristics and achievements.

Important achievements include ***conservation***, which is the ability to understand that the properties of objects remain the same despite changes in their form. This is something that the pre-operational child cannot understand but which can be understood by the concrete operational child.

When a row of buttons is made longer by increasing the space between the buttons the ***pre-operational child*** would say there were now more buttons in the row. The ***concrete operational child*** would recognise that the number of buttons had been conserved, despite the increased spacing. Therefore the stretched-out row of buttons still had the same number of buttons in it.

Conservation

Piaget's Conservation of Number: The increased spacing between each button in the lower row does not prevent the child from recognising there are the same number of buttons in each row.

The Importance of Piaget's Work

Piaget developed his theories and conducted his experiments when American psychology was predominately behaviourist in orientation. He kept alive and developed a cognitive approach to the mind long before the cognitive revolution, described in Chapter 3, had occurred. Piaget had no access to the neuroimaging technology described in Chapter 4, so he was unable to correlate his results with neurological data. Nevertheless, his work is still highly influential both in academic psychology and in education and pedagogy. While some of his explanations have been questioned, the experimental data he obtained from his children is still researched and investigated in contemporary psychology.

He developed his theories before the information processing approach was developed and before neuroimaging allowed us to examine the functioning of the brain. Contemporary ***developmental psychologists*** are attempting to bring this all together.

SOCIAL CONSTRUCTIONIST APPROACHES TO DEVELOPMENT

One criticism of Piaget's theory of cognitive development is that he neglected or underplayed the role of culture and social interaction. Lev Vygotsky (1896–1934) drew on Marxist thinking to put social interaction at the heart of cognitive development in a bid to provide a historical materialist account of child development. For Vygotsky, cognitive development was synonymous with socialisation or *enculturation*. To become an independent individual capable of private thought was an achievement that depended on joint action with others. He argued that language is fundamentally a social phenomenon and that thought is simply internalised speech.

Lev Vygotsky believed cognitive development depended on socialisation.

Vygotsky said that *pre-speech*, the natural babbling of an infant, is interpreted and directed by the caregivers. In the joint activity of conversation, this pre-speech becomes less one sided. Caregivers might begin by correcting the vocalisations of infants and finish older children's sentences until they learn to make fully formed utterances. Children then speak aloud to themselves in order to regulate their own behaviour and eventually this speaking aloud is internalised and what was once public speech is now inner thought. The general direction in Vygotskian theory is from the social to the individual.

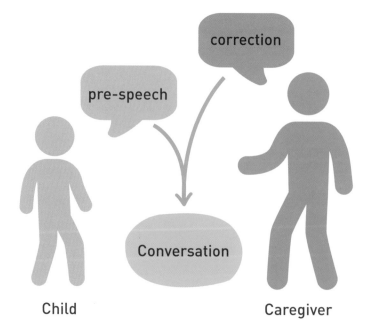

correction

pre-speech

Conversation

Child   Caregiver

Vygotsky argued against the idea that scientific thinking was the natural end point of cognitive development. He argued that science was a specific cultural invention and that different cultures and societies developed cognitive tools to solve their particular problems.

During the process of *enculturation* the child is faced with problems set by their physical and social environments. Initially, children can't solve these problems on their own but they can solve them with the aid of a caregiver or teacher. These problems belong to the *zone of proximal development* (ZPD). They are the primary site of cognitive development. This is because once the skills and capacities that are demonstrated in the joint activity with the more capable partner have been achieved the child is then ready to move on and solve even more complex problems.

Zone of proximal development

Cannot be solved.

Can be solved with the help of a teacher – zone of proximal development.

Can be solved on their own.

ZONE OF PROXIMAL DEVELOPMENT ▶ *problems that a child can solve only with the help of a teacher.*

Scaffolding and the Spiral Curriculum

Jerome Bruner (1915–2016) was an American social and developmental psychologist who borrowed from both Piaget and Vygotsky to develop influential models of teaching and learning. From the theory of the ZPD he developed the idea of **scaffolding**. Here the teacher takes children to the limits of their current ability and supports their problem solving through joint action until they can solve the problem on their own; the teacher then removes the support. Rather than 'stages', Bruner referred to **different modes of representation**. These are:

- action based (enactive)
- image based (iconic)
- language based (symbolic)

As understanding grows, these forms of representation of a particular knowledge domain become better integrated. His concept of the **spiral curriculum** is an approach to teaching in which the same material is revisited in successively more sophisticated ways, thereby integrating different forms of representation.

Jerome Bruner created the idea of scaffolding, where teachers help their pupils reach the limits of their ability through joint action.

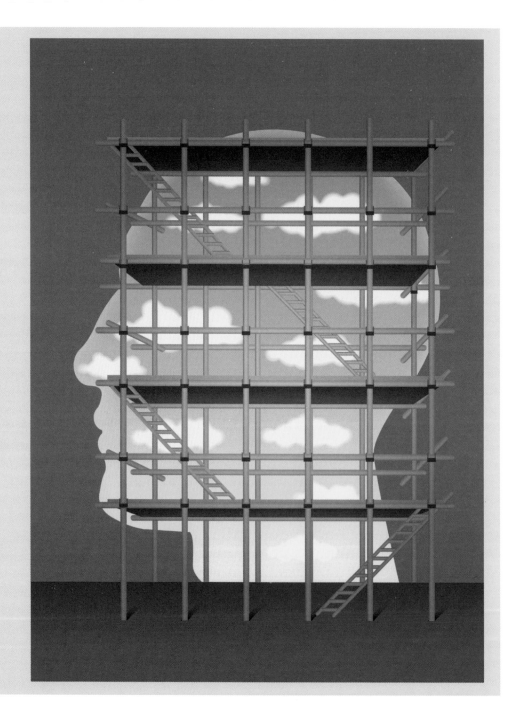

SPINAL CURRICULUM ▶ *teaching the same material by revisiting it in progressively more sophisticated ways.*

Vygotsky and Piaget: A Comparison

Without doubt, Vygotsky and Piaget are still the most influential developmental psychologists. In some respects they are similar. Both stress that activity is the engine of cognitive development. Piaget considered abstract logical thought to be the natural endpoint of cognitive development. On the other hand, Vygotsky, with his roots in Marxism, believed that scientific thought was a very particular cultural achievement and was not an inevitable result. There is a greater stress on culture in Vygotsky's ideas, and less emphasis on a set of invariant stages or universal principles, such as *accommodation* or *assimilation*, in his work.

PSYCHOANALYTIC APPROACH TO DEVELOPMENT

Psychoanalysis offers a model of psychopathology and a general account of the structure of the human mind. It is also a *stage theory* of child developmental (see pages 96–9). Sigmund Freud (1856–1939), the founder of psychoanalysis, believed that, for the neonate, the primary contact with the world is through the mouth. The centre of the baby's life is satisfying its needs by sucking at the breast or bottle. As the baby grows it develops teeth, which opens up the possibility of biting as well as sucking. This stage is known as the 'oral phase'. At around 12 months or so, potty training begins. The child can please or disappoint the caregivers by letting go or holding on to their waste. This adds a new dimension to the infant's relationship with the world and it is at this point that the infant begins to understand that other people exist. At around four years old, children discover their own genitals as a source of pleasure and learn that males and females are anatomically different.

Sigmund Freud

Oedipus complex

This is a key moment in Freud's account because boys now become scared that their genitals could be removed (***castration anxiety***) and girls believe that their genitals have been removed. This is highly controversial and many feminist authors have argued that this account is sexist because it leads to defining femininity as the lack of a penis. The male child deals with castration anxiety by, somewhat paradoxically, trying to become more like his father, who is the prime source of castration anxiety. This process is referred to as the ***Oedipus complex***. After the Oedipus complex is resolved during latency, the child's sexual energy is focused on hobbies and other pursuits. At puberty the sexual energy becomes directed towards members of the opposite sex. Freud identified these stages through his clinical sessions with adult patients in order to understand their personalities. We will return to psychoanalysis in Chapter 9.

Sigmund Freud was the founder of psychoanalysis and offered a form of the stage theory of children's psychological development.

Prenatal Learning

Piaget and Vygotsky began their investigation into cognitive development at birth. In the 1980s, William Fifer and colleagues went even further back, beginning a series of studies of fetal learning:

- DeCasper and Fifer (1980) gave babies the choice of sucking on a non-nutritive nipple that allowed them to hear the voice of their mother or one that provided the voice of a stranger. The babies preferred the one that allowed them to hear their mother's voice.
- Fifer and Moon (1995) gave neonates a choice between their mother's voice heard clearly and their mother's voice muffled so that it sounded as it did in the womb. The neonates preferred their mother's voice muffled.
- DeCasper, Lecanuet, Maugeais, Granier-Deferre and Busnel (1994) asked mothers to read a story aloud three times a day four weeks before the baby was due to be born. Two weeks before the due date, tape recordings of the mother reading the story and reading a new story were played to the foetus in the womb. The fetus's heart rates dropped when the familiar story was played, indicating that they recognised their mother's voice.

These studies show that the foetus can learn and that the story of human development begins before birth.

ATTACHMENT THEORY

John Bowlby (1907–90) was trained in both experimental psychology and psychoanalysis. As an upper-class child growing up at the start of the twentieth century, his primary caregivers were a series of nursemaids and nannies. He saw little of his mother and was sent to boarding school at the age of seven where he was intensely miserable. In the 1940s, he studied delinquent children and noticed that, of the forty or so boys he interviewed, half of them had experienced early separation from their primary caregivers. Driven by his own life experiences and his work with troubled children, he began to think systematically about the role of the caregiver and the consequences of separation and loss of the caregiver. He concluded that early social attachment between an infant and a caregiver is necessary for adequate social development.

Bowlby's student Mary Ainsworth designed a structured observation technique called the *strange situation test* in which the primary caregiver and child are placed in a room. After a few minutes the psychologist enters the room and speaks to the caregiver, who then leaves. The child is left alone in the room with the experimenter and then the caregiver returns. Ainsworth was interested in the exploratory behaviour of the child when it was alone with the caregiver, the reaction to the psychologist and the reaction to the caregiver leaving and coming back. More recent work has explored the effect of early attachment behaviour in later life. Research has shown that, among other indices, securely attached children grow up to have higher self-esteem, qualifications and better relationships with their partners and their own children than those who were insecurely attached as children.

John Bowlby

NAMES TO KNOW: OTHER APPROACHES TO DEVELOPMENTAL PSYCHOLOGY

Harry Harlow (1905–81)

John Bowlby (1907–90)

Albert Bandura (1925–present)

Lawrence Kohlberg (1927–87)

SECURE ATTACHMENT	Explores environment with caregiver, distressed when caregiver leaves, delighted when caregiver returns.
INSECURE/RESISTANT	Clings to caregiver, cries when the caregiver leaves, angry when returns.
INSECURE/AVOIDANT	Avoidant: No response when caregiver leaves and no response to caregiver when they return.
INSECURE/DISORGANISED	No consistent pattern of interaction with the caregiver when together and after separation.

The four kinds of attachment Ainsworth identified and the behaviours associated with them.

Harry Harlow and Monkey Love
In the 1950s, Harry Harlow (1905–81) conducted a series of experiments on Macaque monkeys to investigate the effect of early experiences on subsequent behaviour. Under the banner of studying 'monkey love', he designed two kinds of mechanical surrogate mothers. One was made of bare wire mesh and the other of soft flannel. He found that, even when milk was supplied from the wire surrogate mother, the infant monkeys would spend more time nestling into the soft surrogate. He concluded that the monkeys were seeking 'contact comfort' and this was more important than the simple satisfaction of nutritional needs. In further experiments he brought up some monkeys without a source of contact comfort. He found that this early experience severely affected subsequent development and, these monkeys never developed good social skills.

In his experiment, Harry Harlow created 'surrogate mothers' for the monkeys.

Social Learning Theory

The theories we have looked at have examined global theories of cognitive and emotional development. In the 1960s, Albert Bandura conducted a series of studies that examined how children learn from others. In these experiments, children were exposed to adults (male and female) acting aggressively (hitting a self-righting doll called a Bobo doll) and non-aggressively (ignoring the Bobo doll). The children were roused by showing them attractive toys and then telling them they couldn't play with them. In another room containing more toys their behaviour was observed. Those children who had been exposed to the adult acting aggressively imitated the aggressive behaviours they had observed. Those who were exposed to the non-aggressive behaviours were significantly less aggressive. There were also some sex differences with female children being influenced more by male actors. Overall, the boys were more physically aggressive than the females. The study demonstrated the power of imitation on the behaviour of children. Some of these toys were categorised as non-aggressive (plastic animals and crayons, for example) and others as aggressive (a dart gun and a toy hammer).

Albert Bandura designed an experiment using Bobo dolls to examine how children could be influenced by the actions of adults.

MORAL DEVELOPMENT

While it is true to say that Piaget was not uninterested in moral development, his primary focus was on cognitive development. Lawrence Kohlberg (1927–87) spent much of his career looking at how children grow up to understand the concept of right or wrong and to hold different attitudes to societal norms and laws. He borrowed from Piaget in terms of his methodology and produced a stage theory of moral development with some parallels with Piaget's theory of cognitive development. Kohlberg's method was to present children of different ages with a series of moral dilemmas where there was no definitive right or wrong answer. As Piaget before him, he was interested in the reasoning behind the child's choice rather than the conclusion the child came to.

Lawrence Kohlberg developed a theory describing how children learned the concept of right and wrong.

One of the most discussed dilemmas described a dying woman who could be saved by a newly invented drug. The husband of the dying woman, Heinz, pleaded with the drug's inventor to sell him the drug at an affordable price but the inventor refused because he wanted to get a good profit from his hard work. None of Heinz's friends could lend him the money to buy the drug so

LEVEL	AGE RANGE	STAGE	NATURE OF MORAL REASONING
Level I: Preconventional Morality	Starts in early childhood.	**Stage 1**: Punishment-avoidance and obedience.	Decisions are made on the basis of their consequences.
		Stage 2: Self-interest.	Willing to cooperate with others if there is some personal gain.
Level II: Conventional Morality	Appears around age 6–8. Seen in a few older elementary school students, some junior high school students, and many high school students. (Stage 4 typically does not appear until the high school years).	**Stage 3**: Good boy/ girl.	Decisions are made on the basis of authority. The primary desire is to please the powerful. Those with less power than oneself do not need to be considered.
	Appears around 15.	**Stage 4**: Law and order.	Rules need to be followed and shouldn't be questioned.
Level III: Postconventional Morality	Rarely seen before college. (Stage 6 is extremely rare, even in adults).	**Stage 5**: Social contract.	Rules are recognised as being made by people and subject to change if they no longer benefit us.
		Stage 6: Universal ethical principle.	One's conduct must be governed by one's conscience, which itself is the result of rational reflection on the principles we freely choose to live by.

Stages of moral development with their associated types of moral thinking.

Heinz had to decide whether or not to break into the laboratory to steal the new drug or watch his wife die. The children were asked what Heinz should do and to explain their answer.

Kohlberg carried out a longitudinal study (testing and retesting the same participants over an extended period) and identified three levels of moral thought, each one comprising two stages.

Kohlberg's theory stimulated much debate. One of the criticisms that was levelled at his account of moral reasoning is that he, perhaps, followed Piaget a little too closely. His assumption that the end point of universal ethical principles was equivalent to Piaget's identification of universal abstract thought as the highpoint of cognitive development betrayed a particular cultural bias. The application of context sensitive wisdom gained from examining individual cases might be considered a higher form of morality than following abstract principles. These kinds of debates draw on fundamental issues concerning whether or not psychology is, or could be, or should be, value free. In Chapter 6, Social Psychology, we will briefly return to these issues.

OTHER APPROACHES TO CHILD DEVELOPMENT

In this chapter we have examined the psychological theories that have shaped our understanding of human development. It is now clear that we have to think about studying development from before birth and we have to look at not just cognitive development but also social development and emotional development. We have not been able to look at all the important theories of cognitive development. The theories of cognitive psychology that focus on information processing and the new techniques of brain imaging are promising; they should allow us to understand in greater depth the dynamics of development and their neurological correlates. The scope of developmental psychology is also changing as life expectancy increases and medical intervention becomes more sophisticated. We now have to consider development across the whole life span, not simply stopping at early adulthood. The study of development remains a crucial and challenging part of psychology and that promises to be the case into the future.

DEVELOPMENTAL PSYCHOLOGY

The proper education and socialisation of children was a concern of political theorists and educators. In 1762, Jean-Jacques Rousseau (1712–78) described the 'proper' education of two fictional children, Émile and Sophie, in his work *Émile, or Treatise on Education,* in which he explored the relationship between the individual and society. He argued that education should allow a child to grow and gain independence and develop the resilience not to be corrupted by the adult world. Rousseau's ideas were taken up by educators across Europe, including Johann Heinrich Pestalozzi (1746–1827) and Friederich Fröebel (1782–1852), who then influenced the educator Maria Montessori (1870–1952). These pedagogues believed that the child learns best through activity and play. The study of children as a topic of scientific interest began when, in 1877, two articles appeared in the journal *Mind* by Hippolyte Taine (1828–93) and by Charles Darwin (1809–82). Other 'baby diaries' followed, becoming an essential source of evidence for psychologists studying child development.

Jean Piaget (1896–1980) moved from observation to testing the skills and abilities of his own children. From these controlled observations, Piaget developed genetic epistemology to account for the growth of knowledge from birth to adulthood, publishing *The Language and Thought of the Child* (1923, French version) and going on to write more than 50 books and 500 papers. In the USSR, Lev Vygotsky (1896–1934) investigated the development of higher psychological functions, regarding these functions to be first and foremost cultural inventions that are passed from generation to generation through social interaction. Vygotsky's work was rediscovered in the West in the 1960s. Other traditions have contributed to our understanding of how cognition and emotions change over time but have not drawn on specifically developmental concepts. Instead, they have argued that the differences between adults and children are the result of the increase of information processing power, neural connections, opportunities for associative learning and so forth that occur over time.

Hippolyte Taine was one of many late Victorians who sought to discover through careful observation how children's minds developed.

Chapter Six
SOCIAL PSYCHOLOGY

Völkerpsychologie – Social Psychology of Attitudes – Implicit Associations – Obedience to Authority – Group Performance – Intergroup Conflict – Contemporary Social Psychology

COGNITIVE DISSONANCE

LIKERT SCALE

CARL HOVLAND

CONTEMPORARY TRENDS

SUPERORDINATE GOAL

ATTITUDES

ROBBER'S CAVE

METHODOLOGICAL INDIVIDUALISM

VÖLKERPSYCHOLOGIE

INTERGROUP CONFLICT

REALISTIC CONFLICT THEORY

PREJUDICE

IMPLICIT ASSOCIATION

RICHARD LAPIERE

SOCIAL PSYCHOLOGY

GROUP PERFORMANCE

GROUP THINK

DECISION MODEL

BYSTANDER INTERVENTION

AUTHORITY

STANFORD PRISON EXPERIMENT

ZAJONC'S COCKROACHES

NEGATIVE STATE RELIEF MODEL

OBEDIENCE

STANLEY MILGRAM

SOCIAL IDENTITY THEORY

EICHMANN TRIAL

EXPERIMENT

VÖLKERPSYCHOLOGIE

Most of the topics examined in this chapter come from experimental psychology but we start with a brief examination of the *Völkerpsychologie* approach. As we have already learned, Wilhelm Wundt considered psychology to be the study of conscious experience and to be limited in scope to an examination of simple sensory processes using a method of carefully controlled experimental introspection. He believed that the *higher cognitive processes* that we employ when we engage in institutions such as politics, religion, law and the arts can't be understood in terms of the psychological functioning of individuals and argued that two forms of psychology were necessary to understand what it is to be human. This non-experimental psychology he called *Völkerpsychologie* and he took it very seriously, writing 10 volumes on the subject.

Higher cognitive processes

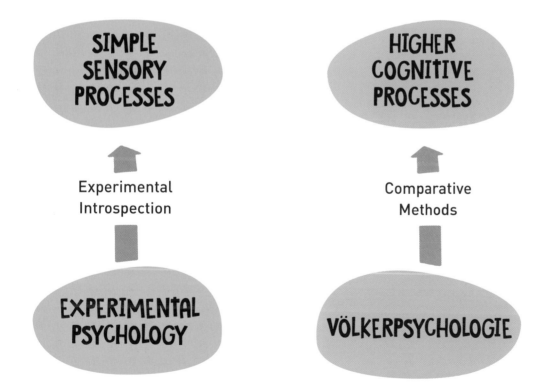

Völkerpsychologie and Sociological Approaches to Social Psychology

Wundt argued that language was fundamentally a social phenomenon in as much as it is not the invention of a single human consciousness. Language and the institutions that rely on language must, according to this view, be understood as connected systems of parts that cannot be reduced to the actions of individuals. Theorists who take this position are arguing against the principle of *methodological individualism*, which holds that all social phenomena can be understood as the summation of the actions of single persons.

However, Wundt's distinction between experimental psychology and *Völkerpsychologie* was ignored by most of those who came after him. When psychologists began to study how groups functioned, social conflicts started and ended, and the effect of other people on an individual's actions, they used methods and theories derived from experimental psychology and theories drawn from first learning theory and later cognitive psychology. Nevertheless, Wundt's argument that social psychology was different from experimental psychology was never totally dismissed and to this day there are psychologists who have tried to keep alive the *Völkerpsychologie* tradition.

METHODOLOGICAL INDIVIDUALISM ▶ *all social phenomena are the summation of the actions of individuals.*

More radical proponents of Wundt's views have taken his arguments further and claim that human consciousness and the use of language have consequences for the way we understand psychology as a science. They argue that language allows us to reflect on ourselves and this introduces a fundamental *reflexivity* to psychological thinking. This, they argue, makes psychology a *human science* rather than a physical science because what is at issue for humans is *meaning* rather than *causality*. According to psychologists such as Ken Gergen (1973), social psychology is more akin to the study of history or, for Rom Harre and Paul Secord (1972), more like anthropology or sociology.

SOCIAL CONSTRUCTIONISM ▶ *psychological concepts are created to support particular modes of social organisation.*

The work of these and others has led to the development of social constructionism. This is part critique of psychologists who 'misunderstand' their own science as a natural science, and part social critique, arguing that psychological concepts like intelligence and depression are not natural categories or concepts but have been created to support particular modes of social organisation. Most psychology courses will discuss these accounts of psychology under the titles of *hermeneutic psychology* or *critical psychology*.

Hermeneutic psychology

THE SOCIAL PSYCHOLOGY OF ATTITUDES

The first major concern of those who called themselves 'social psychologists' was the study of attitudes. In the early 1920s, US psychologists were increasingly keen to apply psychological knowledge to social problems such as racism and the breakdown of communities and families. Early social psychologists chose to approach these problems using the concept of *attitudes*.

Attitudes

ATTITUDES ▶ *a set of preconceptions are involved when individuals interact.*

NAMES TO KNOW: STUDYING ATTITUDES

Wilhelm Wundt *(1832–1920)*

Carl Hovland *(1912–61)*

Louis Thurstone *(1887–1955)*

Rensis Likert *(1903–81)*

Richard LaPiere *(1899–1986)*

Attitudes have been defined in different ways by different researchers. What these definitions share, however, is the idea that when individuals interact they are not simply treating each other as totally unknown beings but bring to the interaction a whole set of preconceptions, feelings, expectations and beliefs. These are, in part, the result of previous direct experience and, in part, the result of what they have learned from their peers, families and social groups. The concept of attitude has thus allowed psychologists to look at the way these various preconceptions lead to bias and prejudice.

115

After spending a huge amount of time and energy measuring attitudes, social psychologists turned their attention to researching how attitudes could be changed. In the early 1940s, Carl Hovland (1912–61), at Yale University, was engaged in work for the US Government to improve the morale of new army conscripts who were being prepared to fight in Europe and Asia. Many of these conscripts had little desire to fight abroad and believed that far-away wars were of no concern to them. Hovland and his team evaluated the 'Why We Fight' series of movies and conducted experimental research to find out the most effective way to deliver persuasive messages. Using the phrase '*Who says what to whom with what effect*' to guide their research, Hovland and his colleagues discovered that attitudes were difficult to alter but using high authority and attractive sources facilitated changes in attitudes.

Carl Hovland used experimental research to find persuasive messages to improve the morale of American soldiers in World War II.

How to Measure an Attitude

In the 1930s, L.L. Thurstone, who contributed to the study of intelligence and personality (Chapters 7 & 8) invented a way of measuring attitudes. They used the responses of many participants to devise scales that indicated where someone was positioned with respect to a particular statement. The method was quite complex and time consuming to follow. In 1932, Rensis Likert invented a simpler method. His invention, the **Likert Scale**, has become ubiquitous in psychological research, opinion poll market research and for entertainment online or in magazines. An example of an item from a Likert Scale designed to measure attitudes to psychology is given below. The full scale would be made up of multiple items chosen on the basis that they discriminate between people with positive or negative attitudes to psychology.

Rensis Likert invented a scale to measure social attitudes that has become ubiquitous.

STRONGLY AGREE	AGREE	NEITHER AGREE NOR DISAGREE	DISAGREE	STRONGLY DISAGREE
1	2	3	4	5

Usually Likert scales have 5 or 7 scale points. Generally speaking, respondents find more scale points confusing (see Chapter 3: Cognitive Psychology and discussion of the limits of information processing). It has been found that it is usually best to have an odd number of scale points so that respondents have the option of giving a neutral response ('Neither Agree nor Disagree'). Participants who are forced to choose between 'Agree' or 'Disagree' may refuse to finish the questionnaire!

LaPiere and the Problem with Attitudes

One of the most famous studies in social psychology was conducted not by a psychologist but by a sociologist. Richard LaPiere was interested in racial prejudice against Chinese workers prevalent on the west coast of the USA during the 1920s. Travelling to hotels with two young Chinese colleagues, he compared the reception they received when they arrived with the initial response he got from the hotel when he first contacted them to say he wanted to stay and bring a Chinese couple with him.

What he found was that the expressed attitude to his phone calls or letters – usually indicating they did not want anyone Chinese staying in their establishment – and the actual response when they arrived was very different. He and his friends were treated very well and, in his estimation, received above average service. LaPiere concluded that what people say (**expressed attitudes**) and what people do (**actual behaviour**) are related in complex ways; it is not a simple direct relationship.

Investigating prejudice in US hotels in the 1920s, LaPiere found that his Chinese travelling companions did not fit the stereotype racist hoteliers expected.

Many of the hotel receptionists or owners he contacted may well have been racists and virulently anti-Chinese. When push came to shove, however, they may have been too embarrassed to refuse service or more interested in filling their rooms than indulging their prejudices. Quite possibly the young couple that LaPiere travelled with did not fit the hotelier's expectations of a typical Chinese person (they were professional and middle class). So, although the hoteliers were still anti-Chinese, the couple were treated well because they did not fit a **stereotype** or collection of beliefs and feelings about a particular category of people or events.

LaPiere's research, as expressed in a 1934 paper, dented the confidence of social psychologists who were studying attitudes to issues such as prejudice. The rationale for studying attitudes in the first place was that they would accurately predict behaviour. If they didn't, what was the point of measuring them? Thirty years later, when Wicker (1969) conducted a meta-analysis (a review that aggregates data from lots of different studies) into this issue, he found that measured attitudes were poor predictors of behaviour. (Specifically, in studies in which attitudes and behaviour had both been measured, the correlation between them was weak – about $r = 0.3$. (see page 143))

IMPLICIT ASSOCIATIONS

LaPiere's account of the questionable relationship between attitude and behaviour was highlighted very early in the history of social psychology. But his finding was discounted and thousands of studies of attitudes followed. As people have been exposed to attitude research and as prejudice and bias towards people of different racial groups has become less and less socially acceptable (and often illegal), there is a genuine worry that when people report their attitudes they are giving socially acceptable responses rather than saying what they genuinely think or feel. For those researching bias and prejudice in society, this is a serious flaw; these studies might not be valid and therefore the conclusions drawn from them false.

The ***implicit association test*** (IAT, Greenwald et al, 1998) was developed to covertly measure attitudes to different social groups. The test is based on the idea that we have unconscious attitudes (that is, attitudes we are not aware of) that shape our behaviour. In the IAT, participants are asked to respond to pairs of concepts. We can respond more quickly to pairs of concepts that we closely associate together rather than to pairs of concepts that we do not closely associate together. For example, one concept might be 'good', which can be elicited with items such as 'joy', 'love' and 'peace'. The conceptually opposite 'bad' can be elicited with items such as 'agony', 'terrible' and 'hurt'.

Implicit association test

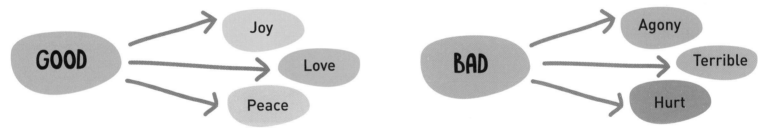

In a study of racial prejudice, these items are paired with faces of black or white people. Someone who is prejudiced against black people responds more slowly when black faces are presented along with 'good' items. By measuring reaction times to these different pairs of concepts, the authors of the IAT believe they have found a way of measuring prejudice or bias that is not affected by social desirability. Critics argue that it has not been empirically demonstrated that these scores are valid nor that there is evidence that slower responses are linked to actual racist behaviour. This is a highly contentious area.

Racial prejudice

To test oneself using the IAT and to learn more about its construction, Project Implicit maintains a website at Harvard University: https://implicit.harvard.edu/implicit/

Cognitive Dissonance

Most of the research on changing attitudes focused on the use of persuasive communications. Leon Festinger (1919–89) stood this on its head by showing that we often change our own attitudes rather than have them changed for us. In a classic experiment, Festinger asked participants to repeat a tedious task that required participants to turn wooden pegs by x degrees again and again. After they had done this, they were thanked for taking part and asked to rate the task on enjoyability, learning, importance and willingness to participate again. They were told the experiment was now officially over but they were asked if they wouldn't mind helping out with participant recruitment because the psychologists were rather shorthanded.

Participants who accepted $1 to lie changed their attitudes in order to help remove the cognitive dissonance they felt.

QUESTION	CONTROL GROUP	$1 GROUP	$20 GROUP
1. How enjoyable tasks were (-5 to +5)	-0.45	+1.35	-0.05
2. How much learned (0 to 10)	-3.08	2.80	3.15
3. Scientific importance (0 to 10)	5.60	-6.45	5.18
4. Participate in similar experiences (-5 to +5)	-0.62	+1.20	-0.25

If they agreed to help out they were told that they should go into the room where potential participants were waiting to take part and tell a 'little white lie'. They were to say to potential participants that the experiment was fun. One set of students was offered $1 for telling this lie, a second set of students was offered $20 and a third set was offered no money at all. After complying with the request, they were asked to re-rate the initial experiment. What was remarkable was that those who had thought the task was boring still thought so even after they had accepted $20 to lie. This was also true of those who were not offered any money. However, those who had accepted $1 to lie now considered the initial task to have been much more enjoyable than before and said they were much more likely to participate than before. According to Festinger, this is explained by **cognitive dissonance**, which is the state we feel when there is a mismatch between our beliefs and actions. Faced with the realisation that they had lied for $1, the participants felt uncomfortable and reduced this discomfort by changing their attitudes. They had not lied simply for $1 but because, on reflection, it was a great task all along. **Cognitive dissonance** theory is an example of a **consistency theory**. According to these theories, a basic human motivation is to maintain the coherence and integrity of our actions and behaviours. If this is disturbed we are motivated to bring them back to a coherent pattern.

COGNITIVE DISSONANCE ▶ *the state of mind when there is a mismatch between our beliefs and actions.*

OBEDIENCE TO AUTHORITY AND SOCIAL INFLUENCE

After World War II psychologists engaged in a great deal of theoretical reflection and empirical research to try to understand and explain the causes of the conflict and especially the Holocaust – the systematic murder of at least six million European Jews. Stanley Milgram (1933–84) was one of these social psychologists. When Adolf Eichmann was tried in Jerusalem in 1961 for his role in the deaths of hundreds of thousands of people, Milgram was impressed by the philosopher Hannah Arendt's observation that Eichmann was not obviously the bloodthirsty, anti-Semitic monster that the prosecution described. No doubt his actions were blood thirsty, monstrous and anti-Semitic but Eichmann came across as a petty bureaucrat who was most concerned with showing how efficient he was to his bosses. Arendt referred to 'the banality of evil' to describe how the actions of people like Eichmann, which are essentially thoughtless, lazy and rather self-centred, can lead to unspeakable crimes. Milgram took this observation to the laboratory and devised one of the most famous experiments in psychology.

Adolf Eichmann provided the classic example of what Hannah Arendt described as 'the banality of evil'.

Stanley Milgram devised an experiment to see how easily ordinary people could commit acts of violence.

Experimenting with Authority

Milgram set up a series of experiments to test Arendt's contention that ordinary people can commit terrible crimes in the name of complying with authority. In these tests, genuine participants were tricked into believing they were experimenters who were testing the memory of another participant, identified as the 'learner'. As 'experimenters', they were asked to administer electric shocks to the 'learner'. These shocks gradually increased in intensity (or so the participants believed) and as the shocks were administered the learner (who was acting the part and who was not visible to the participant), began to cry out as if in pain. It was clear that the 'experimenters' were uncomfortable about continuing to administer electric shocks beyond the pain threshold. They were not threatened or bullied into doing so. It was enough for them to be given the instruction 'the experiment must proceed' by a supervisor to secure their acquiescence. Milgram argued that this demonstrated the power of compliance with authority.

In Milgram's experiment, participants were asked to administer electric shocks to another participant. Most continued to do so even when it seemed clear that the learner was in great distress.

NAMES TO KNOW: UNDERSTANDING AUTHORITY

Leon Festinger (1919–89)

Stanley Milgram (1933–84)

Philip Zimbardo (1933–present)

Milgram and the experts he consulted before the experiment began expected the 'experimenters' to abandon the experiment after administering a few shocks. Most psychologists thought the 'experimenters' would refuse to go on once it became apparent that the learner was in great pain. In the experiment, 65 per cent of participants continued to administer shocks up to the highest intensity. Critics of Milgram's experiment argue that it was unethical to put participants in a position where they thought they were inflicting serious injury on other people.

Philip Zimbardo's studies reinforced how powerful the effect of a situation could be in determining behaviour.

The Stanford Prison Experiment

The powerful effect on people put in positions of power was made apparent in the work of Philip Zimbardo (1933–present). In his 'Stanford Prison experiment', a corridor in the psychology department of Stanford University became the 'prison'. Students were randomly assigned the role of prison guard or prisoner. With no explicit instructions other than to keep order in the 'prison', the 'guards' took their assigned role to extremes and reacted with increasing authoritarianism when the 'prisoners' questioned their behaviour. Guards punished prisoners for offences by making them do push-ups and standing on their backs. On the second day, the 'prisoners' rebelled, and the guards responded with extreme measures – the ringleader was placed in solitary confinement and the other participants were stripped naked. Some prisoners were given special treatment and others punished and a few even began to suffer from mental breakdowns. The guards, so immersed in the experiment, refused to believe these symptoms were real. The experiment was scheduled to run for two weeks but Zimbardo decided to end it on the sixth day when it became clear that the prisoners were suffering physical distress and severe mental trauma.

It has entered the public consciousness, inspiring two movies, *The Stanford Prison Experiment* (2015) and *The Experiment* (2010), a film loosely based on the themes raised by Zimbardo.

GROUP PERFORMANCE

Dating back to the 1890s, studies had shown that the presence of a co-actor can affect an actor's performance (see Chapter 10). Until the 1960s, what was less well understood was how a passive audience rather than a co-actor can affect performance, as research literature up to then was inconsistent. Then Robert Zajonc (1923–2008) conducted a series of experiments in which he varied the difficulty of a task and the presence or absence of an audience. Zajonc showed that when individuals performed tasks that were straightforward and well practised (*dominant responses*) their performance improved when other people were present. When the task was difficult (*non-dominant*), the presence of other people adversely affected their performance. Zajonc inferred from this that we are genetically pre-programmed to become more aroused in the presence of others in order to prepare us to fight or flight. For easy tasks, this readiness to respond enhanced performance; in difficult tasks, however, it interfered with the calm and reflective state needed to deal with complexity.

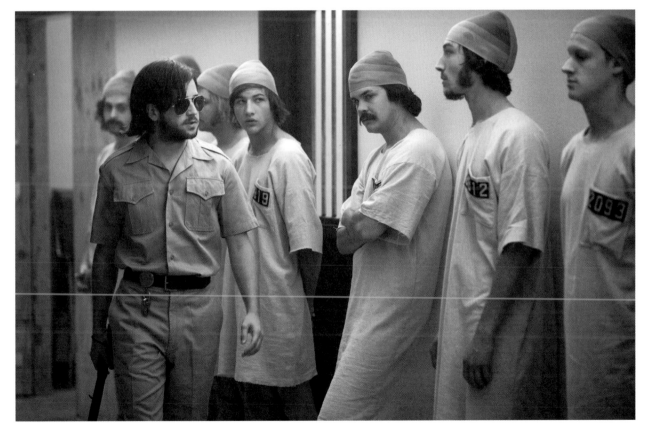

The Stanford Prison Experiment randomly split students into 'guards' and 'prisoners' and found the behaviour of the guards changed rapidly to fit their perceived roles.

Zajonc's Cockroaches
In 1969 Zajonc carried out an experiment in which he explored audience effects with cockroaches rather than human participants! He found that cockroaches performed better in an easy task in the presence of a cockroach audience than when performing a difficult task in front of a cockroach audience. This suggests that these responses are very basic and occur across a very wide range of animal species.

As Robert Zajonc discovered, even cockroaches perform better with an audience.

NAMES TO KNOW: GROUP PSYCHOLOGISTS

Muzafer Sherif *(1906–1988)*

Irving Janis *(1918–1990)*

Henri Tajfel *(1919–1982)*

Robert Zajonc *(1923–2008)*

Bibb Latané *(1937–present)*

John M. Darley *(1938–present)*

So far we have considered group output quantitatively but what about qualitatively? Do groups make better or worse decisions than individuals? In the 1960s, an MIT student, James Stoner, discovered that groups made more risky decisions than individuals, contrary to current received wisdom of the time. A variety of explanations were put forward to explain why groups were making more risky decisions than individuals. Perhaps group membership allowed one to choose a potentially dangerous option because if something did go wrong then the responsibility could be shared across the group? Roger Brown (1925–1997) suggested that it was because American culture valued people who took risky decisions, and when people were put in a group to make a decision they discovered they were actually quite cautious and thus advocated taking more risks to enhance their feelings of self-worth.

Follow-up work showed that groups were not more inherently risky than individuals but that putting people into groups polarised their decision-making. So, individuals who tended towards a risky option became more amenable to risk when put in a group with like-minded people. Similarly, individuals who tended toward less risky options became even more prone to caution when put together with others of the same mindset.

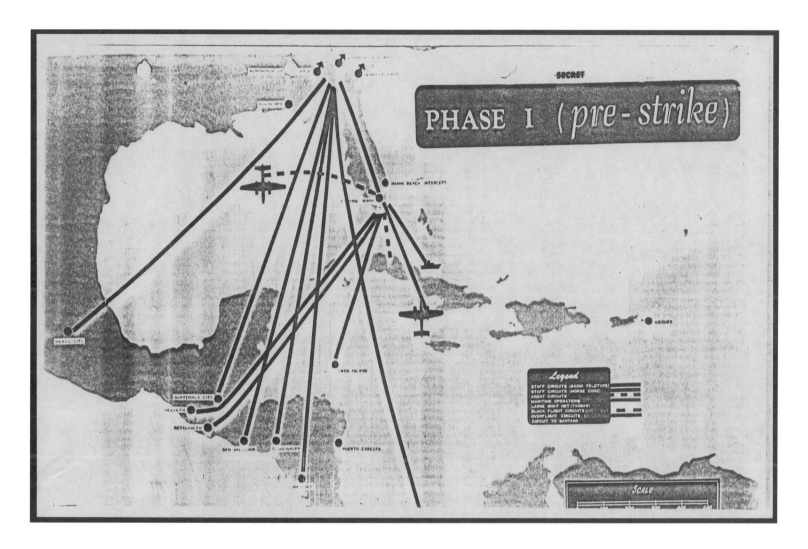

The quality of decision-making and risk-taking was researched further by Irving Janis who reconstructed the processes that had occurred in a number of cases when very poor governmental decisions had been made. These situations included the US Government's support for the Bay of Pigs invasion of Cuba and the Israeli Government's lack of preparation for war in October 1973.

The US invasion of the Bay of Pigs in 1961 is a famous example that demonstrates the danger of group think.

Irving Janis argued that groups often place pressure on dissenting members to conform and they display questionable moral judgement and tend to discount warnings.

GROUP THINK ▶ *groups make more risky, less effective and more morally questionable decisions than individuals.*

Janis argued that these poor decisions had been made because the decision-making group had been subject to a process he called *group think*, which he defined as '*A deterioration of mental efficiency, reality testing and moral judgment that results from in-group pressures*'.

Eight Symptoms of Group Think

- *Illusion of invulnerability* leads to unjustified optimism and risk taking.
- Collective efforts to *discount warnings*.
- Unquestioned *belief in group's morality*.
- *Stereotyped views of adversaries* (too evil to negotiate with, too stupid to be a threat).
- *Pressure directed* at any dissenting group member.
- A shared *illusion of unanimity*.
- *Self-censorship* of deviations from group consensus.
- Self-appointed *'mind guards'* protect group from information that might challenge the complacency.

Four Defences Against Group Think

- The group leader should remain impartial as much as possible.
- The group should actively seek opinions from other people.
- Within the group, sub-groups should be formed that are relatively autonomous from each other.
- Within the group, members should be given the opportunity to state opinions anonymously.

INTERGROUP CONFLICT

Muzafer Sherif (1906–88) argued that the basis of intergroup conflict wasn't fear of people who were different because of their race, religion or ethnicity but because different groups were in competition for scarce resources, such as jobs, access to education and health services.

Sherif's 'Robber's Cave Field' study tested this hypothesis empirically. Sherif showed that competition for scarce resources did indeed produce inter-group hostility. Later researchers discovered that hostility could be produced without any explicit competition. Henri Tajfel carried out a series of experiments in which he demonstrated that simply categorising schoolboys into two groups on the flimsy pretext of which modern artist they preferred was enough to result in positive bias towards an in-group and negative bias towards an out-group.

Tajfel went on to develop *social identity theory*, which argues that all of us have a basic motivation to categorise the social world in terms of group membership and that group membership can carry positive or negative values. If we compare our own membership of different groups and overall we belong to low value groups, we are motivated to change the value of those groups. This might be done by changing the way in which we evaluate groups. For example, Tajfel noted that in 1960 American Civil Rights reformers took part in 'Black is beautiful' campaigns to raise the value of black skin colour so that when members of a black in-group evaluated themselves on the value of skin colour their evaluation became positive.

Social identity theory

Many participants in the civil rights movement also took part in the 'Black is beautiful' campaigns.

REALISTIC CONFLICT THEORY ▶ *intergroup hostility results from competition over resources and only the existence of a superordinate goal can restore good relations.*

The Robber's Cave Field Study

Muzafer Sherif emigrated from Turkey to the US in the 1940s. Concerned with inter-group conflict and drawing on Marxist ideas about the economic causes of social conflict, he conducted a series of *field experiments*. In these he used real-life settings to conduct true experiments in which conditions were changed and the effects measured without the participants realising they had been manipulated. At the Robber's Cave park, two groups of boys chosen for their similarity in background and experience were set in competition for small prizes. He observed that the competition soon got out of hand, with the two groups fighting and increasingly treating each other in terms of their group membership rather than as other very similar schoolboys. Even getting the boys to mix while watching a movie and having a meal did not improve group relations. Indeed, the contact between the two groups increased conflict, with a full blown food fight developing at lunch. What did decrease conflict was making the boys believe that they would soon have to leave the camp because the supply truck had broken down and the water tank was damaged. All the boys were enjoying their time at camp and all the boys would have to go home if these problems were not resolved. By getting the two groups to work together, the broken down truck and damaged water tank were fixed. As the boys believed this had enabled the summer camp to carry on, inter-group relations improved and conflict was decreased. Sherif argued that the competition for scarce resources had developed into conflict resulting in hostility. By introducing a *superordinate goal*, that is a goal that was greater than the goals of the two separate groups, the interests of the two groups became intertwined and conflict reduced.

In the Robber's Cave experiment, conflict between the two groups of boys continued to increase until a greater goal was introduced that forced them to work together to achieve it.

> ## SUPERORDINATE GOAL ▶ *a goal common to groups who are in conflict over the pursuit of less important goals.*

Helping Behaviour

Social psychologists have been concerned not just with finding out why people harm each other but also in promoting helping behaviour. In part, this was stimulated by the tragic case of Kitty Genovese who was murdered in 1964 after being repeatedly attacked. These attacks were heard by neighbours who did nothing to help her. Original reports suggested that 38 people heard Kitty being attacked but this was an exaggeration. It is likely that only one or two people realised she was being attacked and did not seek help. However, this was enough to stimulate research into helping behaviour. A short *New York Times* video remembering Ms Genovese can be found at https://www.nytimes.com/2016/04/11/us/remembering-kitty-genovese.html

Reports suggested that 38 people heard the report of the attack on Genovese, but none sought help.

Latané and Darley (1979) proposed a *decision model of bystander intervention* that explained the processes that caused this lack of intervention and the barriers that needed to be overcome before an individual would intervene and help someone.

▶ *Notice the event.*

▶ *Interpret the event.*

▶ *Assume responsibility.*

▶ *Choose how to help.*

▶ *Implement the decision.*

Psychologists such as Daniel Batson (1943–present) have emphasised the empathy altruism – when we see someone in trouble our empathy is aroused and we help. In contrast, the *negative state relief model* – observing someone in trouble – makes us feel uncomfortable and we decide to help in order to get rid of this unpleasant feeling.

NEGATIVE STATE RELIEF MODEL ▶ *seeing someone in trouble makes us uncomfortable, so we intervene to remove this feeling.*

CONTEMPORARY SOCIAL PSYCHOLOGY

This chapter has examined some of the most important research traditions in social psychology including the study of attitudes, group performance and inter-group conflict. The scope of social psychology also embraces topics as diverse as social influence, conformity, inter-personal attraction and inter-personal understanding and misunderstanding. Increasingly social psychologists are working to understand how perspectives are drawn from our understanding of cognitive psychology, neuroscience and sociology in order to develop a full understanding of our place in the social world.

SOCIAL PSYCHOLOGY

Social Psychology occupies a sometimes uncomfortable position between general psychology and sociology. As a branch of general psychology, social psychology has borrowed from first learning theory and then cognitive psychology. Early social psychologists such as Floyd Allport (1890–1979) believed that social psychology was the study of individuals and how by changing individual behaviour you can change behaviour across society. Floyd published *Social Psychology* (1920), one of the first textbooks on the subject. Floyd and his brother Gordon (1897–1967) were instrumental in making the study of attitudes central to social psychology; they investigated measurement in the 1930s, change in the 1940s and their structure in the 1970s. By the 1970s, social psychologists were beginning to investigate how people think about other people under the title of 'social cognition'. This resulted in the identification of how social thinking may be biased. In the 1940s, Kurt Lewin (1890–1947) fled Nazi Germany and began researching group dynamics. As a gestalt psychologist, he believed that putting people into groups produced structures that could not be predicted from the behaviour of individuals. This form of sociological social psychology led to important work on leadership climates and social change. Social psychology is subject to 'crises'. In the 1970s and 80s, this was a crisis of confidence in experimental methods, research ethics and how to understand the relationship between the individual and society. Key figures during this crisis were Rom Harré (1927–present) and Serge Moscovici (1925–2014). Post crisis, social psychology split into different factions. Kenneth Gergen (1935–present) has advocated that social psychology be reinterpreted as social constructionism. Ian Parker (1956–present) has argued that social psychology must be more politically relevant and become a form of critical psychology. Increasingly, social psychologists are embracing qualitative methods to understand human interactions. These qualitative methods include *grounded theory*, based on the sociological method of Barney Glaser (1930–present) and Anselm Strauss (1916–96), and *interpretive phenomenological analysis*, developed by Jonathan Smith, currently based at the University of London.

Rom Harré was a leading figure in the crisis of social psychology in the 1970s.

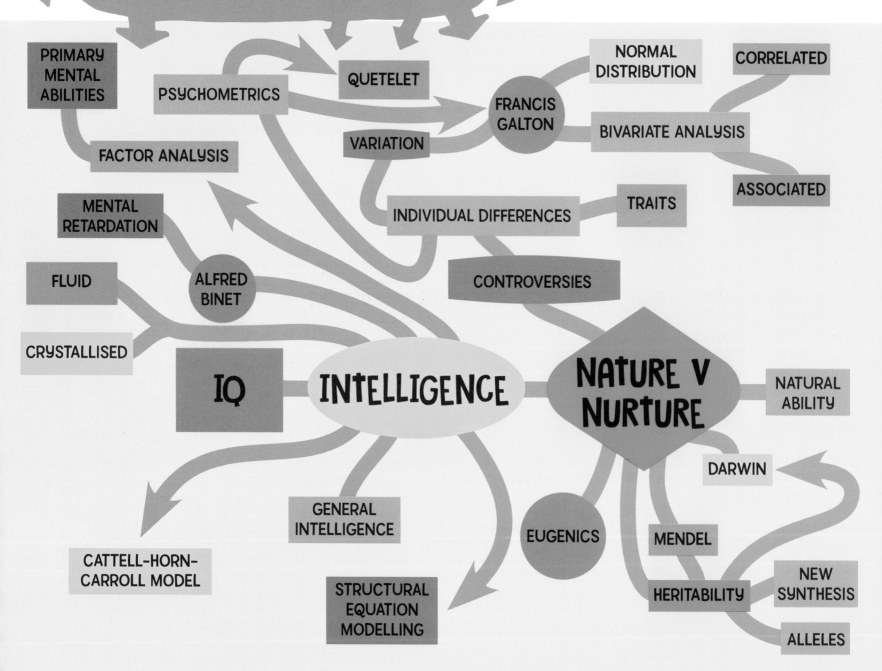

Chapter Seven
THE PSYCHOLOGY OF INTELLIGENCE

Human Abilities and Personality – Measuring Difference – Measuring Intelligence – Charles Spearman and Factor Analysis – Other Models – Future Directions

PRIMARY MENTAL ABILITIES

PSYCHOMETRICS

QUETELET

NORMAL DISTRIBUTION

CORRELATED

FRANCIS GALTON

BIVARIATE ANALYSIS

VARIATION

FACTOR ANALYSIS

ASSOCIATED

MENTAL RETARDATION

TRAITS

INDIVIDUAL DIFFERENCES

FLUID

ALFRED BINET

CONTROVERSIES

CRYSTALLISED

IQ

INTELLIGENCE

NATURE V NURTURE

NATURAL ABILITY

DARWIN

GENERAL INTELLIGENCE

EUGENICS

MENDEL

CATTELL-HORN-CARROLL MODEL

HERITABILITY

NEW SYNTHESIS

STRUCTURAL EQUATION MODELLING

ALLELES

HUMAN ABILITIES AND PERSONALITY

When psychologists study individual differences (the field is sometimes referred to as differential psychology) they assume that people differ in lots of ways and that the ways in which they differ can be studied *systematically*. They aim to reduce the vast complexity of human variation by explaining the source of that variation in a limited number of relatively enduring qualities or characteristics. These are referred to as *traits*. The approach is quantitative and proceeds by constructing scales or tests. The use of quantitative methods to construct tests is known as the *psychometric method*.

TRAITS ▶ *enduring patterns of human behaviour.*

This focus on difference and variability is in stark contrast to the interests of the cognitive psychologists and developmental psychologists that we examined in Chapters 3 and 5. Cognitive psychologists are primarily concerned with identifying and understanding processes that are *common* to all of us.

Cognitive psychologists

For example, the memory researcher is interested in identifying the structures and processes that underlie remembering and forgetting. They posit mechanisms and structures that include long-term memory, short-term memory, semantic memory and episodic memory. When cognitive psychologists conduct a memory *experiment,* they wish to discover what is common to everyone, using the experimental methodology (see Chapter 3) to carefully discount individual differences.

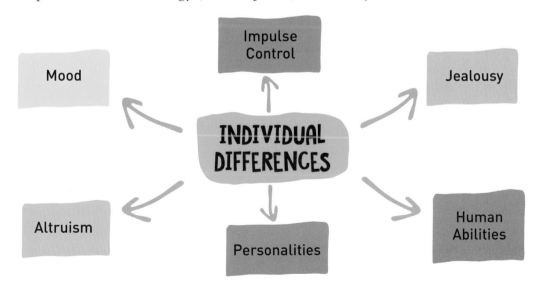

Psychometrics

Under the title of individual differences/differential psychology, researchers have investigated phenomena as wide ranging as mood, impulse control, jealousy and altruism. However, by far the most theoretically and methodologically important areas of research have concerned human abilities and personality. Keep in mind that the psychometric approach taken by differential psychologists to study these areas is the one also used to investigate other psychological phenomena.

Even if you are not concerned with human abilities or personality, it is important to understand the basic measurement principles employed by psychometricians. These are relevant whenever psychologists measure psychological constructs.

'Health Warning'

Any account of the psychological approach to individual differences/differential psychology needs a 'health warning'. This is because the study of individual differences can be traced back to attempts in the nineteenth century to build a so-called 'science of **eugenics**', the goal of which was to improve the overall 'fitness' of the human race. This often involved encouraging, discouraging or even coercing people to breed according to a broad plan. Allied to this concern with selective breeding was the belief that groups of humans could be sorted, primarily by ethnicity, into discrete races and ordered in terms of intellectual and moral superiority. Scores on tests of ability have been used to justify this belief. Many of the key thinkers who were instrumental in inventing the field of individual differences and developing psychometric and statistical techniques were avowed eugenicists and many of them were scientific racists.

THIRD INTERNATIONAL EUGENICS CONGRESS, NEW YORK CITY, AUGUST 21–23, 1932
Introductory Wall Panel "The Relation of Eugenics to Other Sciences," based on a paper by Dr. Harry H. Laughlin, Cold Spring Harbor, Long Island, New York

The study of individual differences began with the more unsavoury 'science' of eugenics.

MEASURING DIFFERENCE – SIR FRANCIS GALTON

Sir Francis Galton was variously an explorer, biologist, inventor, statistician, meteorologist and evolutionist. Our interest here focuses on his work in the fields of statistics and biology and how he put the two disciplines together to define human ability as an object of study with a newly invented set of statistical tools.

The Normal Distribution

Below is a photograph of army recruits who have been sorted out into rows based on their height. On the very far left there is a very short recruit who stands 4 ft 10 in tall (147 cm). On the very far right there is a soldier who stands 6 ft 2 in (188 cm) tall. The distribution of the soldiers from shortest to tallest is not random. Most of the recruits are between 5 ft 5 in (165 cm) and 5 ft 11 in (180 cm) with a few shorter and a few taller.

This distribution resembles the curved shape of a bell. Galton was not the first person to notice this characteristic distribution of height. In 1835, Adolphe Quetelet analysed data from army recruiting centres, had seen the same bell-shaped curve and identified that it approximated the *normal distribution* (also known as the *Gaussian distribution*).

Sir Francis Galton created a crucial set of statistical tools with which to examine human difference.

NORMAL DISTRIBUTION ▶

A symmetrical distribution in the shape of a bell curve with data points clustered around the centre (mean).

4:10   4:11   5:0   5:1   5:2   5:3   5:4   5:5   5:6   5:7   5:8   5:9   5:10   5:11   6:0   6:1   6:2

The army recruits of Connecticut State College in 1914 were lined up according to their height. The resulting photo showed a normal distribution curve.

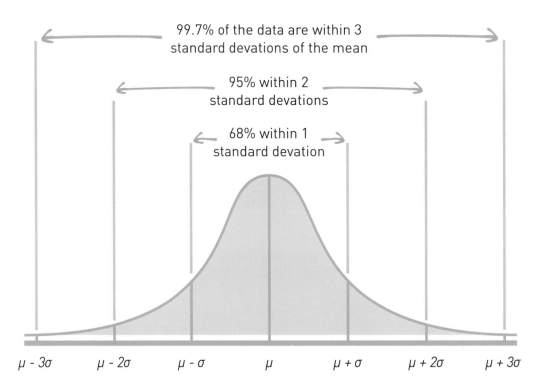

A Normal Distribution shows a bell curve, with most data collected around the mean.

99.7% of the data are within 3 standard devations of the mean

95% within 2 standard devations

68% within 1 standard devation

μ – 3σ   μ – 2σ   μ – σ   μ   μ + σ   μ + 2σ   μ + 3σ

Adolphe Quetelet believed that the variation in heights represented 'mistakes' of reproduction.

For Quetelet, the range of heights seen in the 'normal distribution' was the result of mistakes during reproduction. Quetelet believed that the mean height of a population represented the 'best' or 'healthiest' height and that deviation below or above the mean was therefore the result of error. Drawing on the work of his cousin Charles Darwin's theory of descent with modification to explain the evolution of species, Galton argued that natural variation and natural selection were the basic mechanisms of evolution. Rather than representing errors or providing clues to the 'ideal mean', the variation and individual differences were respectable and essential objects of inquiry in themselves.

BIVARIATE ANALYSIS ▶ *the analysis of the relationship between two variables.*

Scatterplots

Galton extended Quetelet's analysis of single, normally distributed variables such as height and began to examine the relationship between *two* variables, thus inventing *bivariate analysis*. Still considering height as a variable, Galton considered its relationship with another physical characteristic: head size.

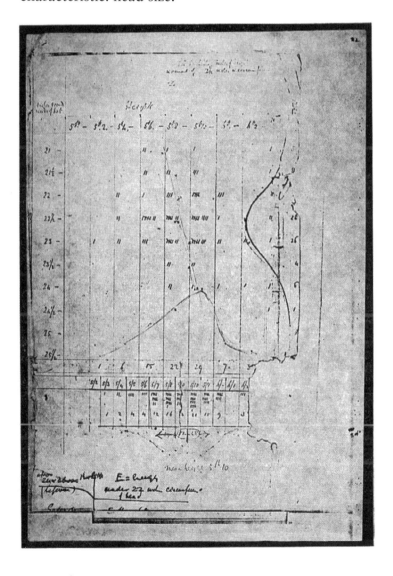

NAMES TO KNOW: STATISTICAL PIONEERS

Adolphe Quetelet (1796–1874)
Normal Distribution

Sir Francis Galton (1822–1911)
Bivariate Analysis and Scatterplots

Karl Pearson (1857–1936)
Pearson Product Moment

This is the first record of a *scatterplot* and represents one of Galton's early attempts to examine how variables are related or, in the terminology that Galton *adopted*, associated or *correlated* with each other. What we can see in the diagram is that height and head size are both approximately normally distributed and when the height of each individual is plotted on one axis and their head size is plotted on the other the pattern shows the greatest density of observations around one standard deviation above and below the mean.

Galton's attempt to graph the relationship between height and head size, the first record of a scatterplot.

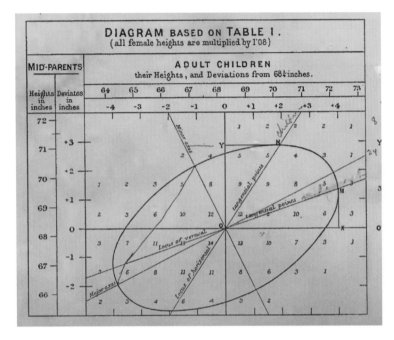

SCATTERPLOT ▶ *a graph that shows the strength of relationships between data.*

In this scatterplot, the height of children is plotted against the difference between the height of the child's father and mother. This bivariate plot shows that although there are some people who have slightly above average head sizes and slightly below average heights, overall as head size increases so does height. Galton did not have the mathematical know-how to quantify the relationship demonstrated in this graphical form but his student, Karl Pearson did.

The bivariate plot shows the heights of children plotted against the difference in height between the mother and father.

Karl Pearson invented the Pearson Product Moment Correlation.

PEARSON PRODUCT MOMENT CORRELATION ▶ *a coefficient that indicates the magnitude of the relationship between two variables.*

In 1895, Pearson invented the correlation coefficient (*Pearson product moment correlation*), which provides us with an indication of the magnitude of the relationship between two variables. Two variables that increase or decrease in exact step with each other have a correlation of +1 and -1. Variables that are unrelated have a correlation of 0. Below are scattergrams illustrating the bivariate relationships for four different data sets with correlation coefficients ranging from -1 to +1.

Pearson product moment correlation

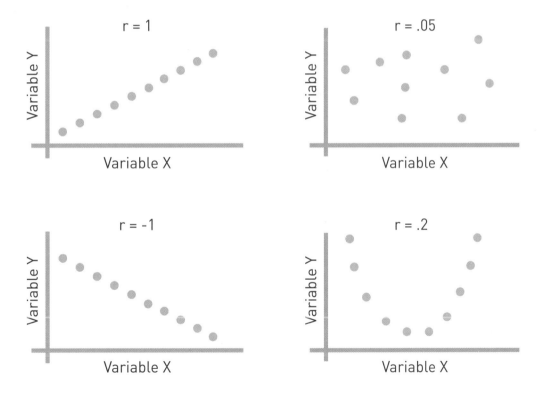

These scattergrams show the bivariate relationships for four different data sets with correlation coefficients from −1 to +1.

Controversy

The study of individual differences in height is not particularly controversial. What is controversial is that Galton took these insights drawn from height and other physical human characteristics such as weight, shoe size and length of bones and argued that they could be applied to *behavioural* characteristics.

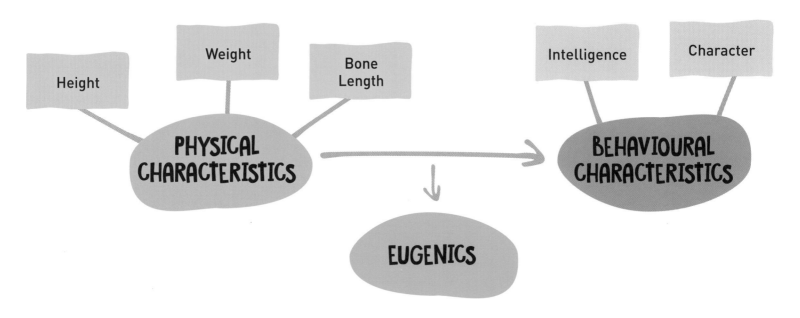

It is here that we see the influence of his ideas about social class and racial differences coming into play. Galton believed that social success was a manifestation of 'natural ability' of 'genius' and was subject to the same mechanisms of natural variation and natural selection that had produced different species. He mapped his own family history and those of other eminent families to demonstrate that genius was passed on from one generation to another.

Testing for 'natural ability'

Galton died in 1911, endowing University College, London, with the funds to pay for a Galton Chair of Eugenics. The empirical study of 'genius' and 'natural ability' had not been successful in underpinning Eugenics, but conceptually Galton provided a blueprint for future research by pioneering the use of tests and correlational analysis.

MEASURING INTELLIGENCE

In France, a stream of thought that would eventually influence the psychological study of individual differences started when Alfred Binet was tasked with devising a means of identifying children who could not cope with mainstream education. Binet rejected Galton's use of physical measures to identify genius or natural ability and turned to the expected school performance of children of different ages. By comparing actual performance with the expected performance of similarly aged children, he was able to diagnose whether a child's academic performance was in line with, ahead of or behind other children.

Alfred Binet

Alfred Binet looked to the school performance of children, rather than physical measures, to determine their intelligence.

Examples of tasks, published by Binet and his colleague Simon in 1905, that children aged 3, 4 and 5 can typically complete correctly.

TASKS	AGE 3	AGE 4	AGE 5
	1. Points to nose, eyes and mouth.	1. Repeats sentence (6–8 syllables).	1. Copies square.
	2. Knows sex.	2. Repeats 3 numbers.	2. Triple order.
	3. Names knife, key, penny.	3. Counts 4 pennies.	3. Repeats sentence (12 syllables).
	4. Gives name and surname.	4. Compares lines.	4. Answers questions. (Comprehension)
	5. Picture-enumeration.	5. Compares faces.	5. Repeats 4 numbers.

The child's scores on the tasks could then be used to calculate their mental age and this could be compared with their actual age. A child who lagged two years behind in terms of their performance compared with other children of their actual age was considered to be retarded by two years.

Intelligence Quotient (IQ)

Instead of the concept of mental retardation, Terman borrowed the concept of *Intelligence Quotient* (IQ) from William Stern. This standardised judgements of performance by dividing the mental age by the chronological age and multiplying the result by 100. If your actual performance is the same as your expected performance, no matter what your age, the Intelligence Quotient (IQ) would be 100.

INTELLIGENCE QUOTIENT (IQ) ▶

$$\text{Intellectual performance} = \frac{\text{Mental Age}}{\text{Chronological Age}} \times 100.$$

The Stanford-Binet Intelligence Test
Binet's tests solved a practical problem in education and were immediately successful. In 1916, at Stanford University, Lewis Terman produced the first edition of the Stanford-Binet Intelligence test, which has been revised and adapted and is still used as a measure of intelligence today.

As new tests have been developed, this standardisation of 100 as the mean IQ has been maintained along with a standard deviation of 15 points. Towards the end of World War I, the American psychologist Charles Yerkes worked with the military to devise tests inspired by Binet to screen army recruits. More than 1.5 million recruits were tested and the results used to allocate the new recruits to different roles.

The Army Alpha used to screen recruits who could read English and the Army Beta used to screen recruits who could not speak English or were illiterate.

NAMES TO KNOW: TEST SETTERS

Alfred Binet (1857–1911) – Binet-Simon Test (1905)

William Stern (1871–1938) – Intelligence Quotient - (IQ) (1912)

Lewis Terman (1877–1956) – Stanford-Binet Intelligence Test (1916)

CHARLES SPEARMAN AND THE INVENTION OF FACTOR ANALYSIS

As a practical tool for identifying mental retardation and screening adults for military service, IQ tests were a huge success. On a theoretical level, the nature of intelligence wasn't really addressed. In England, Charles Spearman, working in the Galtonian tradition, reconsidered how ability could be measured. He rejected the physical measures and looked at academic performance and problem solving.

Spearman rank order correlation

A talented statistician, Spearman invented a test to measure the strength of association between variables that were not normally distributed or were measured on scales that did not have real zero points. This test is known as the Spearman Rank Order Correlation and is still used extensively by psychologists. In 1904 Spearman published a paper in which he introduced the concept of *General Intelligence* ('g').

GENERAL INTELLIGENCE ▶ *also known as the 'g' factor, it underlies all mental abilities.*

General Intelligence was discovered by analysing the correlations between the performance of schoolboys in a series of assessments. Spearman noted that all the correlations were positive. This indicated, according to Spearman, that all problem solving draws on an individual's general ability. In further analysis, Spearman invented the technique of Factor Analysis. This technique has become the tool of psychometricians to this day and allows the observed correlations between a set of variables to be redescribed in terms of a reduced number of variables that are not directly observed but are inferred on the basis of the analysis. These inferred or latent variables are called 'Factors', hence the name of the technique is *factor analysis*.

FACTOR ANALYSIS ▶ *a technique to redescribe observed correlations between a set of variables in terms of inferred variables.*

	Classics	French	English	Arithmetic	Discrimination of pitch	Music
C		.83	.78	.70	.66	.63
F			.67	.67	.65	.57
E				.64	.54	.51
A					.45	.51
D						.40
M						

This table shows a simplified version of the correlation matrix that Spearman presented in his paper.

Factor Analytic Models of Intelligence

Spearman believed that general intelligence , which he called 'g', was a purely intellectual construct. All problem solving requires the mobilisation of 'g', and tests differed to the extent that they required more or less 'g' to be successfully completed. In the correlation matrix shown above, success in the Classics (Latin and Greek) required a lot of 'g', while music required the least. The path diagram (see page 150) has become popular since the invention of a statistical technique called *Structural Equation Modelling* in the 1970s.

The square boxes are observed/manifest variables (the scores on tests) and the circles are inferred/latent Factors (what explains the patterns of scores). This path diagram shows the general factor 'g' and a whole series of unique factors specific to the test taken. This general factor of intelligence, therefore, is extremely important. If we want to understand someone's intelligence, a measure of 'g' is essential. It is the amount of 'g' available to us as individuals that puts a limit on our intellectual functioning and explains why our performance is better or worse than others.

Structural equation modelling

Spearman's general factor

OTHER MODELS

Spearman's invention of *factor analysis* revolutionised the psychometric approach to understanding intelligence. It did not, however, stop the debate on the structure of intelligence, indeed, quite the opposite. Since Spearman's theory of 'g' was proposed in 1904 and his method of factor analysis first presented, psychometricians have put forward a whole raft of different structures of intelligence.

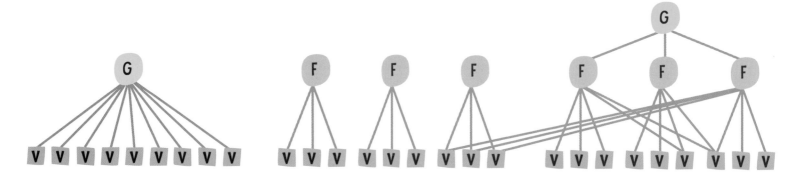

Primary mental abilities

Louis Thurstone (1887–1955) was the first to challenge Spearman. Thurstone argued that 'g' was simply the average of a test battery. When he analysed data from 240 participants who had been given 56 different tests, the best way to describe the pattern of scores was in terms of what he called seven Primary Mental Abilities (PMAs) (see box). For Thurstone, measuring a general factor of intelligence was a mistake. Instead, if we want to understand performance we would need to measure each of these seven PMAs.

Louis Thurstone found seven Primary Mental Abilities that made up intelligence.

Fluid and Crystallised Intelligence

The unitary nature of 'g' came under further scrutiny when, in the 1940s, Raymond B. Cattell argued that psychometric data showed that general intelligence needed to be understood in terms of two separate but related factors: *fluid intelligence* (Gf) and *crystallised intelligence* (Gc).

Primary Mental Abilities
- *Verbal Comprehension*
- *Word Fluency*
- *Inductive Reasoning*
- *Spatial Visualisation*
- *Number Facility*
- *Associative Memory*
- *Perceptual Speed*

Fluid intelligence is a general ability to discriminate and perceive relations. It maps on to Spearman's notion of 'g'. It increases until adolescence and then slowly declines.

Crystallised intelligence is the result of what we have learned over a lifetime and is largely based on the operation of **fluid intelligence**. It is maintained throughout the lifespan.

The Cattell-Horn-Carroll Model

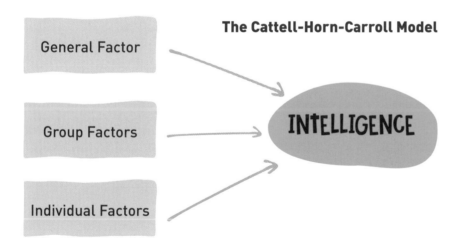

NAMES TO KNOW:
THEORIES OF INTELLIGENCE

Charles Spearman (1863–1945) – *General Intelligence*

Louis Thurstone (1887–1955) – *Primary Mental Abilities*

Raymond B. Cattell (1905–1998) – *Fluid and Crystallised Intelligence*

In 1904, Spearman was arguing that we can account for variation of intelligence by measuring 'g'. More than 100 years later, the current psychometric understanding of the structure of intelligence is that we must understand intelligence as a more complex pattern of abilities and skills.

INTELLIGENCE AND HERITABILITY

The fossil record provided Darwin's evidence for natural diversity, but the mechanism by which physical characteristics were passed on remained a mystery.

Darwin's evidence for descent with modification to explain natural diversity came from examining the fossil record, the study of the development of different species in areas that were geographically isolated, and from the study of the domestication of animals and the selective breeding of livestock to produce cows that produce more milk, hens that produce more eggs and dogs that are better suited to herding sheep or hunting foxes. However, no one understood the actual physical mechanisms by which characteristics could be passed on from one generation to another. The genetic basis of inheritance was yet to be discovered.

Galton looked for evidence for the heritability of talent by searching out genealogical records

of his own family and trying to show that eminence and talent 'ran' in families. His followers accepted his contention when they shifted from eminence to human ability and intelligence.

In 1866, Mendel discovered the basic rules of inheritance that explained how discontinuous characteristics could be passed on to offspring by experimenting with the selective breeding of pea plants and studying qualitative characteristics, such as seed covering (smooth or wrinkled) and flower colour (pink or white). Through his experiments he demonstrated that each parent supplied a genetic element (the *allele*) to their offspring. The two sets of alleles inherited from the two parents (the *genotype*) result in the characteristics that we observe in the offspring (the *phenotype*).

NAMES TO KNOW: INHERITING INTELLECT

Charles Darwin *(1809–82)*
– Natural Selection

Gregor Mendel *(1822–84)*
– Alleles and Mendelian inheritance

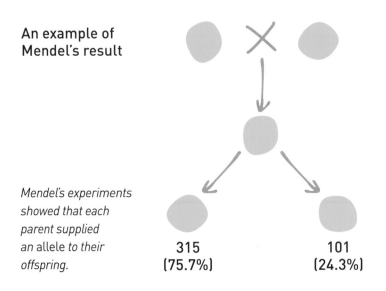

An example of Mendel's result

Mendel's experiments showed that each parent supplied an allele to their offspring.

315
(75.7%)

101
(24.3%)

These alleles are either dominant or recessive. A dominant allele always produces a particular phenotype. A recessive allele is 'switched off' in the presence of a dominant allele and so its phenotype is masked (but not lost). Depending on whether, for example, 'wrinkled skin' or 'smooth skin' alleles are dominant or recessive, the phenotype we observe will have wrinkled or smooth seed. Mendel discovered that in the first generation of offspring only the dominant phenotypes appeared. This is because each plant had one allele from each parent and the dominant one always predominated. But in subsequent generations the recessive phenotype would reappear, wherever the genotype in the offspring had two recessive alleles. Mendel was lucky to have chosen relatively simple characteristics to study. Subsequent studies have shown inheritance to be more complex than this – known as the *'new synthesis'* – but the basic dominant/recessive model still holds true.

The New Synthesis

In the 1930s, the so called *'new synthesis'* demonstrated that when a phenotype is the result of not just one pair of alleles but a whole series of alleles the resulting distribution of phenotypes more closely approximates the normal distribution. This is shown below for the distribution of phenotypes with one pair, two pairs and three pairs of alleles.

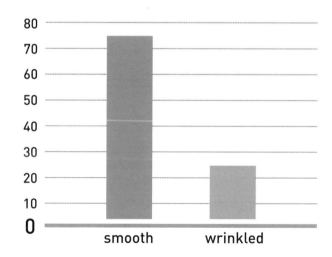

This diagram shows the ratios of wrinkled and smooth-skinned seeds we would expect to see if Mendel's model is correct. Mendel's pea breeding experiments showed the expected ratios.

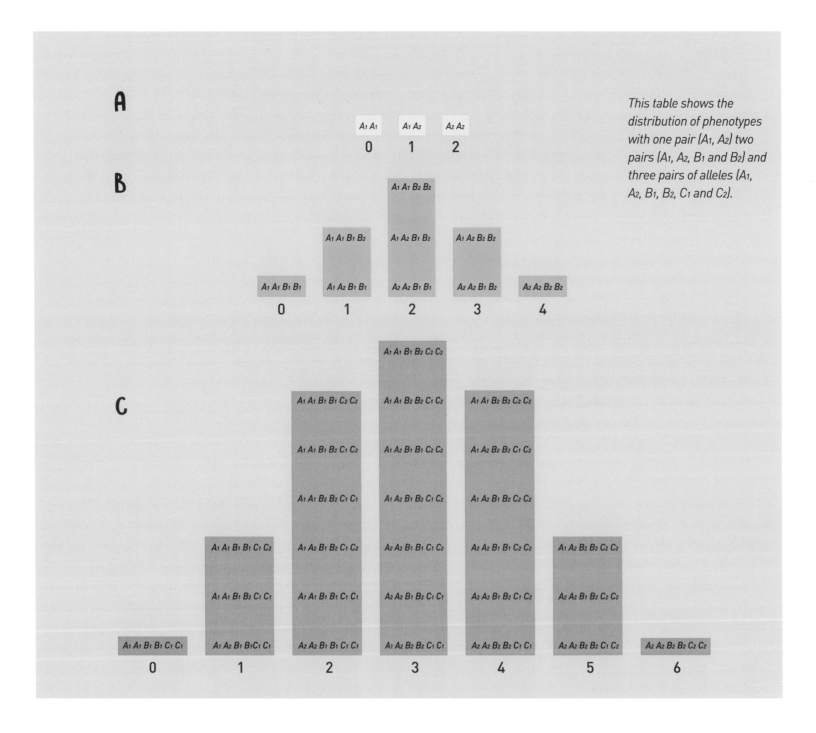

This table shows the distribution of phenotypes with one pair (A_1, A_2) two pairs (A_1, A_2, B_1 and B_2) and three pairs of alleles (A_1, A_2, B_1, B_2, C_1 and C_2).

The 'new synthesis' reconciled the Mendelian account of discontinuous variation (that is, how the alleles for smooth or wrinkled seeds were passed to the next generation) with the continuous variation of characteristics such as human height and – according to the followers of Galton – intelligence seen in the population. It did address the question of just how *much* of the variance of a particular characteristic was passed on between one generation and the next. To address this question of **heritability**, researchers investigated the concordance between scores on intelligence tests and known genetic similarity.

RELATIONSHIP AND DEGREE OF SHARED GENES

12.5% great grandfather	12.5% first cousin
25.0% grandfather	25.0% uncle/aunt
50.0% father	50.0% brother
Me	100.0% identical twin
50.0% daughter	
25.0% granddaughter	25.0% nephew/niece
12.5% great-granddaughter	12.5% great nephew/niece

The study of identical (monozygotic) twins who had been adopted by different families took on a particular importance because these individuals shared the same genetic material but had been exposed to different environments. Since the 1920s, these 'adoption' designs have been a mainstay of estimating the heritability of intelligence. Reviews by Erlenmeyer-Kimling and Jarvik in the 1960s, and Bouchard and McGue in the 1980s estimated that around 50 per cent of the variation in intelligence test scores can be accounted for in terms of differences in genetic material. This research has been highly controversial and has been attacked from different directions.

The Critics

Flynn argues in his book *What is Intelligence? Beyond the Flynn Effect* (2007) that the tradition of measuring 'g' and assuming that estimates of the heritability of intelligence remain constant are a mistake. He argues that there are interactions between brain and environment and that to start to fully understand intelligence it is necessary to consider:

- mental acuity (more or less fluid intelligence)
- mental habits (the way in which we might become better at solving puzzles with practice and increased familiarity)
- attitudes (we have to take a problem seriously if we are going to see it as worthwhile spending time and energy trying to solve it)
- our stock of knowledge that we can bring to a problem
- how quickly we can process information and
- memory (how we access our stock of knowledge).

FUTURE DIRECTIONS

For some psychometricians the measurement of 'g' is one of the twin triumphs of modern psychology (see *The Scientific Study of General Intelligence: Tribute to Arthur R. Jensen* by Helmuth Nyborg published in 2003) while the other triumph is identified as Jensen's persistence in researching 'g' despite constant criticism. For other theorists, for example, Keith Stanovich in his book *What Intelligence Tests Miss: The Psychology of Rational Thought* published in 2009 IQ tests are fundamentally limited because they measure performance on basically abstract puzzles and do not address overarching human rationality which involves selecting actions to help one achieve one's life goals. Put bluntly, Stanovich argues that being 'smart' doesn't necessarily require high IQ and 'clever' people can do dumb things and an adequate account of intelligence should be able to account for this distinction.

It is unlikely that debates about the use and meaning of IQ test scores will be resolved in the foreseeable future. The psychometric research programme, as illustrated opposite, is being further elaborated. This diagram shows how differences in social intelligence (social success) are explained in terms of differences in IQ which are, in turn, explained by differences in neural functioning. Neural functioning has been measured in a number of ways including nerve conduction velocity (NCV) which is an index of the speed of neural functioning, Average Evoked Potential which is a measure of the amplitude of the electrical response of the brain to a stimulus and simple and choice reactions times (RT and CRT) which measure time taken to respond to stimuli. In this model the ultimate explanations of social intelligence are to be found in biology and the direction of causality is from biology to IQ scores to social intelligence. If all else is held constant, differences in underlying biology predict differences in social intelligence; faster and more efficient brains lead to higher IQ scores and higher social intelligence.

Hans Eysenck articulated this model more than 30 years ago. Recent developments in molecular genetics and brain imaging are providing new methods to test the relationship between brain functioning and IQ. Richard Haier in his *The Neuroscience of Intelligence* published in 2017 summarises his own research in this area but note that at this point little of this work has been successfully replicated. Other developments focus on the genetic basis of differences in IQ. Molecular genetics allows research to identify alleles of different genes and test whether particular alleles are associated with high or low IQ scores. Again, little of this work has been replicated and although many candidate genes have been identified, so far no particular gene has been conclusively identified as contributing to variation in IQ scores.

Eysenck's (1998) model of the relationship between biological, psychometric and social intelligence

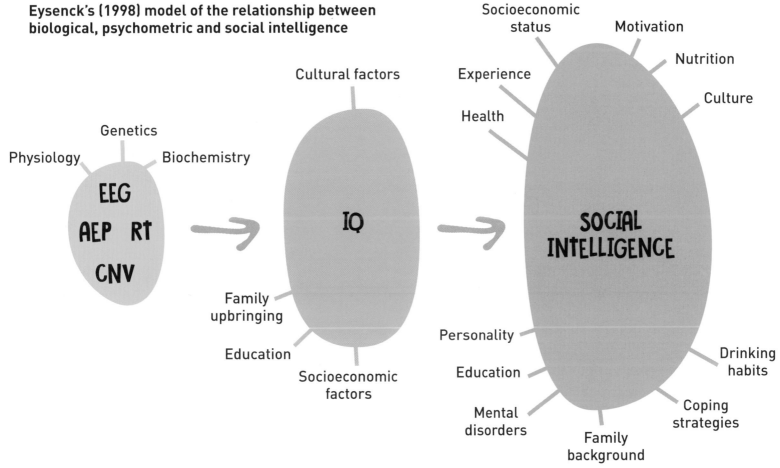

THE PSYCHOLOGY OF INTELLIGENCE

Sir Francis Galton's (1822–1911) studies of hereditary genius laid the ground for the psychometric study of intelligence. The psychometric approach assumed that reliable and valid measures of intelligence could be constructed, scores on these tests were normally distributed and the magnitude of relationships between test scores and performance could be assessed using Karl Pearson's (1857–1936) *product moment correlation coefficient* and Charles Spearman's (1863–1945) *rank order correlation*.

Most psychometricians followed Galton in believing that differences in intelligence were the result of genetic differences. Galton proposed that a new science called *eugenics* could be developed in order to use psychometric evidence to advise on selective breeding programmes to raise the intelligence of the general population. Spearman went on to invent the method of factor analysis in 1904, which built on the method of correlation to provide a means of identifying latent factors underlying patterns of observed scores. Over the twentieth century, different latent factor structures were identified, with Spearman's theory of general intelligence emerging as the most influential.

Historically, psychometric approaches to intelligence and experimental investigations of problem-solving had little overlap. Towards the end of the twentieth century, the two approaches have become more integrated as researchers attempt to support their theories with evidence, drawing on a wider variety of methodologies. In the 1960s, the psychometric approach was challenged on both methodological, theoretical and political grounds. Critics such as Stephen Jay Gould (1941–2002) argued that the concept of intelligence embraced by psychometricians was too narrow. Gould and his colleagues said that the psychometricians had never shaken off their eugenic roots. Throughout the 1970s and 1980s, debates about the status of intelligence became highly politicised, played out in the pages of the *Wall Street Journal* when, in 1994, a group of psychometricians issued the statement 'Mainstream Science on Intelligence', arguing for the scientific respectability of IQ research.

Francis Galton was one of the founders of the psychometric study of intelligence, but he was also responsible for developing the so-called 'science' of eugenics.

Temperament, Character and Personality – Trait Theories of Personality – Raymond Cattell and the Nomothetic Ordering of the Personality Sphere – Hans Eysenck and the Causal Approach to Personality – The Five Factor Theory of Personality

NOMOTHETIC

IDIOGRAPHIC

SELF-EXPRESSION

SOCIAL ADAPTABILITY

TRAITS

RORSCHACH INK BLOTS

FIVE FACTOR THEORY

CONFORMITY

SIR FRANCIS GALTON

EMOTIONAL CONTROL

LEXICAL HYPOTHESIS

PERSONALITY

INQUIRING INTELLECT

GORDON ALLPORT

RAYMOND CATTELL

RELIABILITY

TESTING

16PF TEST

VALIDITY

BIOGENIC THEORY

PSYCHOTICISM

EYSENCK PERSONALITY QUESTIONNAIRE

IMPULSE CONTROL

INTROVERSION

STABILITY

EXTRAVERSION

NEUROTICISM

TEMPERAMENT, CHARACTER AND PERSONALITY

When we talk about other people we have at our disposal a huge range of adjectives to describe how they do things. Someone might be friendly when we ask for directions to the bus stop while the person we asked earlier might have answered aggressively with a curt 'no'. Could we expect the friendly person at the bus stop to be friendly if we bumped into them in a coffee shop and spilled their latte? As well as adjectives to describe behaviour, we also have a huge range of nouns to attribute long-term dispositions to other people. If the person is friendly at the bus stop *and* at the coffee shop, we would be inclined to believe that they are a friendly person and we might refer to their friendly *character*. Are they generally sociable, easy-going, warm? We might talk about their temperament: laid back, sanguine, cheerful. Increasingly, the term we use to describe these enduring dispositions is *personality*. This is the term popularised by psychologists who have tried to map the personality sphere and measure its various aspects.

PERSONALITY ▶ *the enduring qualities of people.*

TRAIT THEORIES OF PERSONALITY

The fundamental assumption of personality theorists is that there is a consistency in the ways in which individuals react to other people and events across time and in different situations. We might like to think that we are unpredictable but personality psychologists are convinced that we are remarkably dependable and uniform in our behaviour.

IDIOGRAPHIC ▶ *concerned with uniqueness.*
NOMOTHETIC ▶ *finds general laws.*

Psychologists understand these consistencies in personality in terms of *traits*. Traits are understood as enduring dispositions to act or respond in certain ways. In the 1920s, Gordon Allport at Harvard University launched the first university course devoted to this subject entitled: 'Personality, Its Psychological and Social Aspects'. Allport's preferred approach to personality was to study an individual in great depth. He introduced the terms *idiographic* and *nomothetic* to distinguish his approach (*idiographic*), which is concerned with uniqueness, from those who were searching for general patterns and laws found across groups of people (*nomothetic*).

Allport popularised the study of personality but his way of trying to find the traits that best describe a particular person in all their specificity never really took off. Instead the *nomothetic* approach to personality took over.

Gordon Allport introduced the terms idiographic and nomothetic to the study of the individual.

Traits and the Lexical Hypothesis

Allport drew on the work of Sir Francis Galton, who we met in the previous chapter, to identify personality traits. In 1884, Galton wrote a paper with the title 'Measurement of Character' in which he listed all the words related to character he could find by looking through sets of dictionaries. From these he made a list of over a thousand words. Using dictionaries and thesauruses to find words related to a particular subject is known as the *lexical approach*. This assumes that language has developed over time to provide us with all the distinctions we need to understand each other and our differences. Allport carried on with this dictionary work and in 1936, with his colleague Henry Odbert, published an extended list of 4,505 trait terms. For Allport, these trait names were the raw material for understanding *individual* cases. For Raymond B. Cattell (1905–98), however, they were a starting point to identify the traits shared by everyone and to produce the most simple and economic way of mapping human personality.

LEXICAL APPROACH ▶ *using the dictionary and thesaurus to find traits related to personality.*

The lexical approach involved creating a list of words from a dictionary to define personality traits.

Trait terms

NAMES TO KNOW: IDENTIFICATION OF PERSONALITY TRAITS

Sir Francis Galton *(1822–1911) – 1,000 trait terms*

Gordon Allport *(1897–1967) – 4,505 trait terms*

Henry Odbert *(1909–95) – 4,505 trait terms*

Raymond Cattell *(1905–98) – 171 trait terms*

RAYMOND CATTELL AND THE NOMOTHETIC ORDERING OF THE PERSONALITY SPHERE

Cattell re-examined Allport and Odbert's list and added specialised terms that came from psychology and psychiatry. He then got rid of synonyms and produced a shorter list of 171 terms. Using these terms, he constructed questionnaires and asked participants to rate themselves on these traits.

Raymond Cattell created a shorter list of 171 trait terms, which he used to create questionnaires.

Personality and IQ tests

In the previous chapter we looked at measures of IQ. Measures of personality are different to IQ measures in some important ways. Someone might score zero on a psychometric test of mathematical ability, indicating absence of mathematical intelligence. When we turn to personality we might describe someone outgoing as an extravert. Someone who is very quiet and shy might be described as an introvert. Introversion and extraversion are polar opposites of the same dimension.

Therefore, a personality test score that indicates introversion may also indicate that someone is not extraverted.

Introversion ⬌ **Extraversion**

IQ and personality tests also differ in the instructions we give to testees. When an IQ test is administered the instructions are to perform as best you can. When a personality test is administered the instructions are to be *honest* in your answers.

Cattell then used the technique of *factor analysis* (FA, see page 174) to identify the pattern of *latent* variables that could explain the pattern of scores.

2ND ORDER FACTORS

Super factors obtained by the FA of the results of FA

SOURCE TRAITS

16 factors underlying personality

SURFACE TRAITS

36 surface traits (correlated but determined by more than one source)

PERSONALITY SPHERE

Allport and Odbert's (1936) list of 17,935 adjectives plus technical terms found in psychological literature.

This diagram shows the structure of personality Cattell identified.

Catell identified 36 surface traits and, underlying them, 16 source traits that he thought were the origin of the different personality patterns we see in everyday life. He argued that these source traits identified by factor analysis and paper-and-pencil tests should also be found in other sources of data. First is a list of things we do (*life record data*) that can be independently verified, such as the number of road accidents we have been involved in, or the number of clubs we have joined. Second are the quantitative tests (*objective test data*) that have an obvious purpose so cannot be faked and which produce directly measureable results.

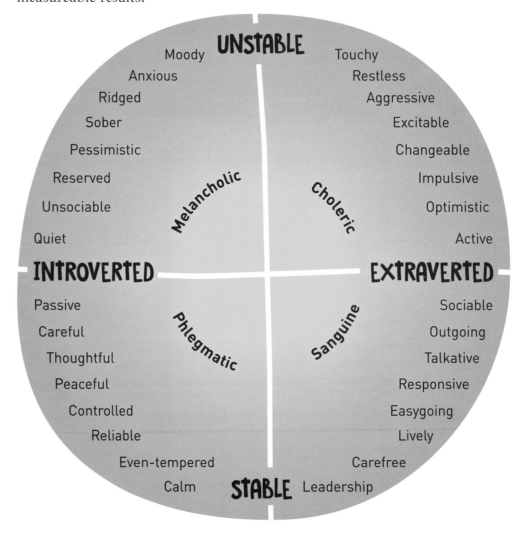

The diagram to the right illustrates the relationship between introversion and extraversion in Eysenck's Theory of Personality.

An example of one of Cattell's objective tests was the 'fidgetometer', which measured 'restlessness'. This was an old chair fitted with electronic contacts that closed as the sitter moved in the chair; the movement was registered on a recording device. This test measured 'restlessness'. On the basis of his research, Cattell published a personality test called the 16PF (Sixteen Personality Factors). This test has been used by career advisors, counsellors and clinicians to provide guidance and as a selection tool. As we shall see, Cattell's theory of personality has been challenged by others working in the lexical tradition and has been superseded by the 'Big 5' approach to personality. But first we will look at an approach to personality that doesn't start with language but which starts with behaviour. This is Eysenck's PEN approach.

16PF test

Items to Measure Personality
Personality tests comprise individual items that go to make up sub-scales that are used to map the personality sphere. For the German-born psychologist Hans Eysenck, for example, the most important aspects of the personality sphere can be captured by three measures:
- *Psychoticism*
- *Extraversion*
- *Neuroticism*

The measures of psychoticism, extraversion and neuroticism (PEN) are sub-scales of the overall test of personality and are made up of a set of items. Generally speaking, the more items in a test (this goes for IQ tests and personality tests) the more reliable will be the measure. Various formats for personality items have been used. Examples of three different formats are shown below:

Item

Check Lists

Forced Choice Format

Hans Eysenck was one of Britain's most acclaimed psychologists.

HANS EYSENCK AND THE CAUSAL APPROACH TO PERSONALITY

Hans Eysenck (1916–97) was one of the most famous and influential psychologists in the UK. Born and raised in Germany, he moved to England in the 1930s where he remained for the rest of his life, contributing to the founding of clinical psychology and the study of intelligence and personality. He began researching personality during World War II when he was working with psychiatric war casualties at the Maudsley Hospital in London. There he developed a scale to measure neuroticism. This scale was further developed by adding a scale to measure extraversion/introversion and published as the Maudsley Personality Inventory.

Over the following decades he conducted further research and analysis, resulting first in the Eysenck Personality Inventory (EPI) and ultimately in the *Eysenck Personality Questionnaire* (EPQ). The EPQ measures three dimensions of personality: extraversion, neuroticism and psychoticism. It also included a 'Lie Scale' which included items such as 'Are all your habits good and desirable ones?' to identify respondents who might be trying to 'fake good'.

At the Maudsley Hospital, Hans Eysenck developed a personality test that measured neuroticism and was later expanded to include the dimensions of extraversion and psychoticism as well.

HANS ENYSENCK'S TESTS

Maudsley Personality Inventory (MPI)

Eysenck Personality Inventory (EPI)

Eysenck Personality Questionnaire (EPQ)

Eysenck's model of personality differs from that of Cattell in that Eysenck started by observing behaviour and its extremes rather than by analysing dictionaries or thesauruses. Eysenck began his research by looking at a clinical population and asking himself how he could understand the differences and similarities within the clinical population and between the clinical population and the healthy population. By the end of his career, Eysenck had produced a biogenic theory of personality that linked differences in behaviour to differences in the functioning of separate neurological subsystems.

Eysenck's Factor Model of Personality

The diagram shows how the dimensions of **neuroticism/ stability**, **extraversion/ introversion** and **psychoticism/ impulse control** are related to each other. Each dimension is orthogonal (90 degrees) to the others, which means they are independent. Scores on one dimension do not tell us anything about scores on the other dimensions.

Autonomous and central nervous systems

The Biogenic PEN model

Eysenck explained individual differences in personality on basic differences in the functioning of three independent biological systems. Differences in neuroticism were the result of differences in the autonomic nervous system (ANS), which is responsible for the unconscious control of a whole host of bodily functions, including rate of breathing, digestion and regulation of heart rate. According to Eysenck, some people have a very sensitive ANS that can change very quickly in response to the internal and external environment (*labile systems*), whereas others have an ANS that is very stable.

Differences in extraversion are the result of different levels of arousability in the *central nervous system* (CNS). Extraverts are typically under-aroused and seek activities that produce more arousal. Introverts are chronically over-aroused and seek calming environments in order to lower their arousal. Eysenck linked the third dimension, psychoticism, with levels of male hormones (androgens). Individuals with high levels of androgens have been shown experimentally to be more aggressive.

Ancient Theories of Temperament

The study of temperament was first used in a medical context, drawing on the ancient theories of Empedocles *c.*450BC, Hippocrates *c.*400BC and Galen *c.*AD150. The ancient Greeks believed that the cosmos was made up of four elements: air, earth, fire and water, and that these were reflected in the composition of our bodies and in our temperament. This theory argued that our temperament reflects the balance of our bodily humours. Someone dominated by blood is described as 'sanguine'. Someone dominated by black bile is 'melancholic'. This theory explains what today we would think of as clinical categories and itself became a part of our language – melancholic, meaning sad, and sanguine, meaning hopeful.

Hippocrates was an ancient Greek physician who believed that our temperament reflected the balance of our bodily humours.

COSMIC ELEMENT	PROPERTY	HUMOUR	TEMPERAMENT
AIR	Warm and moist	Blood	Sanguine (hopeful)
EARTH	Cold and dry	Black bile	Melancholic (sad)
FIRE	Warm and dry	Yellow bile	Choleric (irascible)
WATER	Cold and moist	Phlegm	Phlegmatic (apathetic)

Other Approaches to Measuring Personality: Ink Blots

The most popular way to measure personality is the questionnaire, but other ways have been developed. Hermann Rorschach (1884–1922) believed that when we encounter the world we bring to it our personal pattern of conscious and unconscious needs, fears and desires of which we are often unaware. He invented a test to bring this personal pattern out into the open. The material chosen for the test was intentionally ambiguous so what is revealed says more about us than the test material itself. This test is the famous Rorschach ink blot test and comprises ten symmetrical inkblots:

- 5 are black & white
- 2 black, white & red
- 3 multicolour.

Respondents are asked what the ink blot might be and their responses are written down. The test is scored by looking at the location, the part of the inkblot described, the popularity of the response and the content of the description, such as people, animals and bodily fluids. The Rorschach ink blot test is rarely used in academic psychology but still has its supporters in a clinical setting. In terms of the psychometricians' standards of reliability and validity it fairs quite poorly (see pages 179–81). Rorschach's Inkblot Test is an example of a ***projective test***. Projective tests draw on psychodynamic theories of the mind (see Chapter 9) which assume that there are psychological processes which are unconscious. these unconscious processes are not directly accessible but might 'slip out' or 'colour' our responses to apparently unconnected material. Another well known projective test is the ***Thematic Apperception Test*** invented by Henry Murray (1893–1988). In this test, respondents are asked to look at ambiguous pictures, for example a boy gazing at a violin, and asked to what had lead up to the boy looking at the violin, and what would happen later.

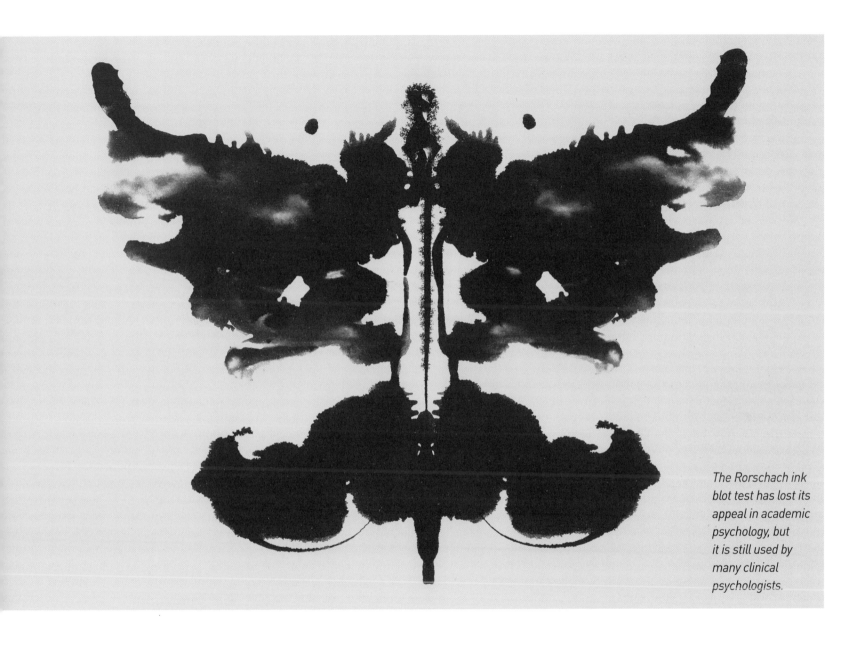

The Rorschach ink blot test has lost its appeal in academic psychology, but it is still used by many clinical psychologists.

THE FIVE FACTOR THEORY OF PERSONALITY

In the late 1940s, Donald Fiske was working for the Veterans Administration on a project to identify and select candidates suitable for clinical training. They began their work by asking candidates to rate themselves using simplified versions of the 16PF. They also asked the candidate's peers to rate the candidates using the same adapted 16PF scales. What Fiske found was that when he ran a *factor analysis* of his data he could not find the 16 source traits that Cattell had found and considered to be the basis for individual differences in personality. What Fiske found was that his data could be best understood in a model that comprised five personality dimensions. These dimensions he labelled as *confident self-expression, social adaptability, conformity, emotional control* and *inquiring intellect.*

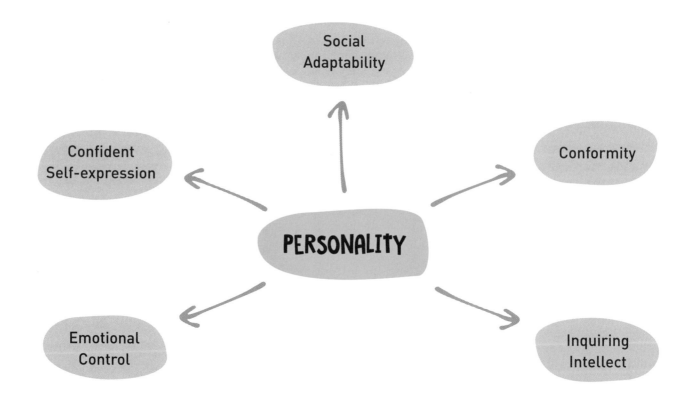

Other researchers, such as Tupes and Christal (1961), and Norman (1963), came up with similar findings. They too could not *replicate* or recover Cattell's 16PF pattern but they did find the same five dimensions – or at least very similar dimensions – that mapped very well on to those found by Fiske. By the start of the 1960s, factor analysis, which was a complicated and incredibly time consuming and laborious process when carried out by hand, could be done easily by computer. In the 1970s and 1980s computing power increased dramatically, which not only allowed the analysis of huge data sets, but also provided the potential for combining old data sets and reanalysing them. New statistical techniques such as *Structural Equation Modelling* were developed, which allowed researchers to test specific hypotheses and attempt to confirm that particular structures were better than others at explaining variation in a data set.

In this context, Norman revisited the word lists produced by Allport and Odbert in the 1980s, as did Golberg, and they began a new programme to identify the dimensions that best captured the personality sphere, starting from first principles just as Cattell had done 40 years previously.

FIVE FACTOR THEORY ▶ *The five traits of openness, conscientiousness, extraversion, agreeableness and neuroticism explain the differences in the way people behave.*

Again, the five factor pattern was the best way to understand the data. By the end of the 1980s, a consensus began to emerge that these five, very broad factors, or dimensions, represented a reliable finding in personality research. These five dimensions were named 'The Big Five', and *Five Factor Theory* (FFT) has become the most dominant theory of personality in contemporary psychology.

The Big 5

OPENNESS	CONSCIENTIOUSNESS	EXTRAVERSION	AGREEABLENESS	NEUROTICISM
Curious	Organised	Sociable	Soft-hearted	Worrying
Creative	Reliable	Active	Helpful	Nervous
Original	Hardworking	Talkative	Gullible	Emotional
Imaginative	Self-disciplined	Person-orientated	Trusting	Insecure
Unartistic	Aimless	Reserved	Cynical	Calm
Unanalytic	Unreliable	Sober	Rude	Relaxed
Conventional	Lazy	Aloof	Ruthless	Unemotional
Narrow	Careless	Quiet	Irritable	Secure

The Five Factors Today

A number of different tests or instruments are now available to measure the Big Five. These include relatively long tests such as Costa and McCrae's NEO–PI–R (Neuroticism–Extraversion–Openness–Personality Inventory–Revised) which is made up of 240 items, and shorter measures such as Saucier's Big Five mini-markers, which is made up of 40 items. The internal reliability of these tests is high with estimates of reliability well above correlations of 0.7. While it is true to say that the Big Five/Five Factor Theory is easily the most often used approach in psychometric personality, there is still room for further research and debate about the status of the five factors. An assumption of the lexical approach is that these five factors have been encoded into language as a means for people to make sense of each other.

In conclusion, the *Five Factor Theory of Personality* has provided a useful framework for organising personality research within the psychometric tradition. It has not completely silenced debate on whether other structures with more or fewer dimensions than the Big Five are more appropriate accounts of the personality sphere.

John Kihlstrom has suggested that the Five Factor Theory can be understood as the five key questions you might want to answer on a blind date.

Blind date questions   John Kihlstrom has gone so far as to suggest that we can think of the Big Five dimensions as answering what he calls the 'Big Five Blind Date Questions'. If we go on a date with someone we have never met before, these are the questions we want answering as soon as possible. Going beyond the perils of going on a blind date, answers to these questions have survival value when meeting any stranger and it can be argued that being able to answer these questions confers a survival advantage.

BIG FIVE	BLIND DATE DATE QUESTIONS	SURVIVAL QUESTIONS
Neuroticism	Is he or she crazy?	Is X unpredictable or stable?
Extraversion	Is he or she outgoing?	Is X active or passive?
Agreeableness	Is he or she friendly?	Is X warm or cold?
Conscientiousness	Is he or she reliable?	Can I count on X?
Openness to Experience	Is he or she smart?	Can I teach X?

If it is the case that the Big Five dimensions have been encoded into language because they give us information useful in establishing inter-personal relations, then we would expect the Big Five dimensions to be universal. For example, they would be found in all languages – not just English. It is not beyond the bounds of possibility they would also be found in other species. Indeed, King and Figueredo (1997) asked zoo keepers to rate the chimpanzees in their charge and found differences that mapped on to the Big Five. The most important strategy for demonstrating that the Big Five factors are, indeed, universal has been to examine languages other than English. To begin with, researchers simply translated Big Five personality tests into other languages. This approach can show that the five factors are in the translated language but they cannot show if they are the best way of understanding the target from the 'inside'. To do this, the lexical approach needs to be applied from the beginning and researchers must look at the home language and start with dictionaries compiled in that language. The research so far is not totally conclusive. Angleitner and Ostendorf (1989) successfully recovered the five dimensions in German. Yang and Bond (1992), however, had equivocal success in recovering the five factors in Chinese, although it must be said that the there was considerable overlap.

Reliability

A reliable measure is one that gives consistent results when applied to the same object. A tape measure made out of Plasticine would not be reliable because it could be easily squashed or stretched. It is far better to make a tape measure out of a robust material such as non-stretchy cloth or thin steel. In psychology, the equivalent of choosing the right material to make a tape measure is to go through a thorough period of pre-testing and pilot work. The items that go to make up a finished intelligence test or a personality test have been shown to give consistent results over time and to be measuring the same construct. A good test will have had its reliability measured in a number of different ways that might include:

TEST–RETEST RELIABILITY ▶ *an individual's score on a test should correlate highly with their score on the same test taken at another time.*

INTERNAL CONSISTENCY ▶ *scores on the different items that make up a test should correlate highly with each other.*

PARALLEL FORMS ▶ *if two tests are constructed using the same procedures, scores on the two tests should correlate highly with each other.*

When psychologists choose a personality or intelligence test they will check the reliability in the test manual. The correlation coefficients reported in the manual should be at least 0.7 (a correlation coefficient of 1 indicates a perfect linear relationship and of 0 no linear relationship at all).

Validity

A valid psychometric test is one that has been shown to measure what its constructors claim it measures. An intelligence test would be of no use in measuring personality, for example.

The validity of a psychometric test is measured in a number of different ways. These tests of validity show that the scores on the test are related to other tests and behaviours that would be expected if, indeed, the test was measuring what it was supposed to be measuring. Measures of validity include:

PREDICTIVE VALIDITY ▶ *Scores on the test correlate highly with behaviours related to the underlying construct. Children who score highly on a measure of extraversion find employment as adults in jobs that require social interaction.*

CONCURRENT VALIDITY ▶ *Scores on the test correlate highly with other measures of performance or ability. Teacher estimates of mathematical ability correlate highly with scores on test of mathematical ability.*

Note that the use of intelligence and personality tests is highly regulated. Only qualified psychologists are allowed to buy and use published psychometric tests.

Teachers can estimate the mathematical ability of their students on the basis of their test scores – an example of concurrent validity.

PERSONALITY PSYCHOLOGY

The ancient Greek physician Hippocrates (c.460–c.370BC) identified four *humours* (bodily fluids): yellow bile (a fluid produced by the liver to digest fats), blood, black bile (dark digested blood) and phlegm (a thick substance secreted by mucous membranes), which corresponded respectively to the cosmic elements fire, air, earth and water. Ideally, the cosmic elements and the humours are in balance, giving rise to an individual perfectly adjusted to the world. The dominance of one humour over the others gives rise to four different temperaments: *choleric* (quick to anger, caused by excess of yellow bile), *sanguine* (cheerful, caused by excess of blood), *melancholic* (depressive, caused by excess of black bile) and *phlegmatic* (easy going, caused by excess of phlegm). This theory dominated European medicine and art for centuries.

Other theories that linked the bodily constitution with personality include those of Ernst Kretschmer (1888–1964), who in the 1920s distinguished between 'pyknic' (broad bodied), 'leptosomatic' (narrow bodied) and athletic types, mapping the pynik type to manic-depression and the leptosomatic type to schizophrenia. William Sheldon (1898–1977) argued that the three germ layers that form during embryonic development are related to physical constitution, with *ectomorphs* (thin and delicate and tending to be thoughtful and introverted), *mesomorphs* (muscular and tending to be assertive and active) and *endomorphs* (rounded and tending to be easy going and extroverted).

These constitutional theories of personality were replaced from the 1940s onwards by psychometric approaches to personality developed by researchers who wanted to measure the 'non-intellective' traits that might add to our understanding of human performance. Raymond B. Cattell (1905–98) and Hans Eysenck (1916–97) developed competing psychometric models of personality. Today, psychometric approaches to personality are dominated by the 'Big Five theory' or 'Five Factor Model' developed by – among others – John M. Digman (1923–98) and Lewis Goldberg (1932–present).

FLEGMAT SANGVIN

JAELANC COLERIC

The theory that the four bodily humours (yellow bile, blood, black bile and phlegm) determined temperament was widely accepted before the twentieth century.

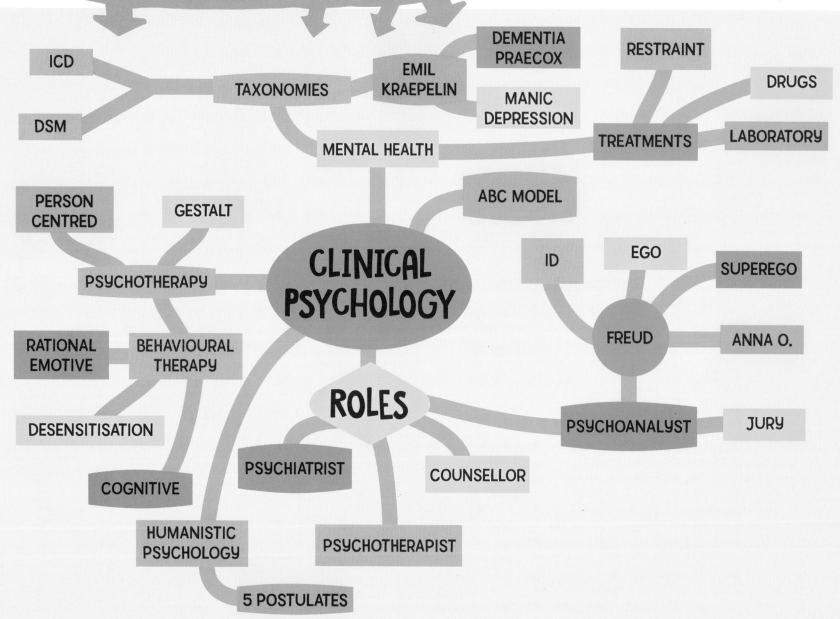

Chapter Nine
CLINICAL PSYCHOLOGY

Psychiatrists to Psychoanalysts – Approaches to Psychological Distress – Psychiatry and the Medical Model – Psychological Approaches to Mental Distress – Humanistic Psychology – The Role of the Clinical Psychologist – Cognitive Behavioural Therapy

ICD

DSM

TAXONOMIES

EMIL KRAEPELIN

DEMENTIA PRAECOX

MANIC DEPRESSION

MENTAL HEALTH

RESTRAINT

DRUGS

TREATMENTS

LABORATORY

PERSON CENTRED

GESTALT

PSYCHOTHERAPY

ABC MODEL

CLINICAL PSYCHOLOGY

ID

EGO

SUPEREGO

FREUD

ANNA O.

RATIONAL EMOTIVE

BEHAVIOURAL THERAPY

DESENSITISATION

COGNITIVE

ROLES

PSYCHIATRIST

COUNSELLOR

PSYCHOANALYST

JURY

HUMANISTIC PSYCHOLOGY

PSYCHOTHERAPIST

5 POSTULATES

FROM PSYCHIATRISTS TO PSYCHOANALYSTS

When we experience psychological distress or just want to try to improve our mental well-being, there is a wide range of different specialists who we can call on to help us. These specialists include:

- clinical psychologists
- psychiatrists
- psychotherapists
- counsellors
- psychoanalysts

The boundaries between these specialisms are sometimes fuzzy, however. Someone who needs psychological help is always best advised to first seek expert advice in choosing which specialist is most suitable for their particular problems.

APPROACHES TO PSYCHOLOGICAL DISTRESS AND MENTAL WELL-BEING

The terms used to refer to psychological distress and mental health changed dramatically over the course of the last 200 years. Histories of 'madness' and 'insanity' reveal horrifying stories of people who have been excluded, punished, imprisoned and even tortured because they were not considered 'normal'. So what is 'abnormal'? Someone may be regarded as 'abnormal' because they are a statistical rarity (a deviation from the normal curve, described in Chapter 7) or because their thoughts and actions challenge the laws of customary behaviour. In *psychiatry*, which adheres to the medical model of health and illness, psychological distress is understood as *abnormal behaviour* or *psychopathology*.

Meaning of 'madness'

ABNORMAL BEHAVIOUR ▶ *any behaviour that deviates from what is considered normal (either due to statistical rarity or deviation from custom).*

The medical model understands psychological distress as a symptom of underlying physiological or physical causes. Psychologists and counsellors are generally more likely to refer to 'mental health' and 'psychological distress'. They view these as problems not so much as the result of illness but as feelings and behaviours that lie on a continuum of varied human functioning. Whether we refer to 'psychiatric illness', 'mental health', 'psychopathology' or 'psychological distress', we are using terms that bring with them a whole set of assumptions and attitudes. In 1961, Michel Foucault published a book in which he traced how the term 'madness' had developed and evolved in Europe from the middle ages and has different meanings in political, religious and medical contexts. This book was translated into English as the *History of Madness* (2006).

Michel Foucault traced the origins of the idea of madness in 1961.

	THEORETICAL PERSPECTIVE	CLIENT GROUP	QUALIFICATIONS
Clinical Psychologist	Draws on a range of psychological theories from learning theory to cognitive psychology.	Wide range of clients referred by other health professionals.	PhD or equivalent specialist qualification in Clinical Psychology.
Psychiatrist	Medical model.	Wide range of clients referred by other medical doctors.	Degree in Medicine and further medical specialisation.
Psychotherapist	'Talking cures', which may be informed by psychoanalysis or humanistic psychology.	Self-referrals and referrals from health professionals.	Specialist training and qualifications in particular therapies.
Counsellor	'Talking cures', which may be informed by psychoanalysis or humanistic psychology.	Self-referrals and possibly referrals from health professionals, teachers, human resource advisors and so forth.	Specialist training and qualifications in particular therapies.
Psychoanalyst	Theories that draw directly from the work of Sigmund Freud.	Self-referrals.	Psychoanalytic training.

A summary of the theoretical background, qualifications and clients that make these specialisms in psychology distinctive.

Diagnostic Categories or Taxonomies

The psychiatric categories that we use today have their roots in the work of *Emil Kraepelin* (1856–1926). From collecting and analysing numerous case histories of psychiatric patients, he concluded that the best way to categorise mental illnesses was to look at patterns of symptoms over time rather than at individual symptoms by themselves. He identified two basic patterns. The first he considered to be a progressive neurodegenerative disease, which he called *dementia praecox* (early onset dementia). The second was a pattern of a cyclic or episodic illness that he called *manic depression*. Dementia praecox was renamed by Eugen Bleuler (1857–1939) as *schizophrenia*. These two broad categories influenced the development of diagnostic schemes for the next 100 years.

Psychiatric categories today owe their existence to the work of Emil Kraepelin.

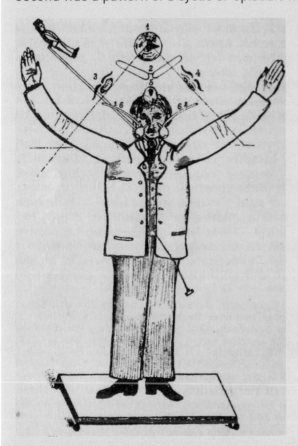

Dementia praecox is better known to us today as schizophrenia.

Today, mental illnesses are diagnosed according to two main taxonomies. The first is the *International Classification of Diseases* (ICD) which began life as the 'International List of Causes of Death', back in1893. The ICD, now in its 10th edition (ICD–10), is a diagnostic classification standard designed to guide clinical work and research. Mental illness was first included in ICD–6 in 1949. The American Psychological Association produced their own version called *The Diagnostic and Statistical Manual of Mental Disorders* (DSM) in 1952. It is now in its fifth edition (DSMV).

These different classifications provide a fascinating window on how the categorisation of behaviour has changed over time. Homosexuality was included as a disorder in the DSM up until 1973, when it was removed after a vote by members of the American Psychological Association. It was only removed from ICD-10 in 1990, seventeen years later than the DSM.

NAMES TO KNOW:
DIAGNOSING MENTAL ILLNESS

Emil Kraepelin (1856–1926)

Eugen Bleuler (1857–1939)

History of
psychiatry

Early psychiatrists
had few effective
treatments and often
resorted to physically
restraining their
patients.

PSYCHIATRY AND THE MEDICAL MODEL

Increasingly, the treatment and management of 'madness' and 'insanity' became the domain of medical doctors who specialised in the treatment of mental illness. Central to the medical model is the contention that these disorders are the result of underlying biological abnormalities. These early psychiatrists (the term is from the Greek for 'mind healers') had few, if any, effective treatments to draw on. Their role was primarily the management of the 'insane', first by physical restraint and then in the second half of the 19th century by drugs such as morphine and potassium bromide. These drugs have been described as 'liquid cosh'.

Advances in medicine during the first half of the twentieth century led to a reduction in the prevalence of mental illness as doctors discovered that many of the occupants of asylums and psychiatric hospitals could be treated and, indeed, cured by simple treatments such as providing better nutrition. For example, pellagra, a disease that resulted in dementia was caused by lack of Vitamin B3 (niacin). In the second half of the century, the discovery and widespread use of antibiotics also dramatically reduced the number of people who were suffering dementia caused by the sexually transmitted disease syphilis, so reducing the population living long term in asylums.

By the end of the
nineteenth century,
drugs containing
potassium bromide
were often used to
manage behaviour.

Before 1850	c.1850–1900	1900–50	1935	1950–present
Physical restraint.	Use of drugs such as morphine and potassium bromide to control behaviour.	Improving nutrition; use of antibiotics.	First lobotomy performed.	Widespread use of drugs to treat symptoms of mental illness.

The twentieth century also saw the introduction of neurosurgical interventions including ***lobotomy*** and ***leucotomy***, which involved cutting the neural connections to the pre-frontal cortex of the brain. This was achieved either by drilling a hole in the skull and inserting a knife or by entering via the eye socket with an implement shaped like an ice pick. These techniques did not 'cure' patients but resulted in them becoming quieter and more 'manageable'. The use of these techniques died out in the 1970s.

Lobotomy and leucotomy

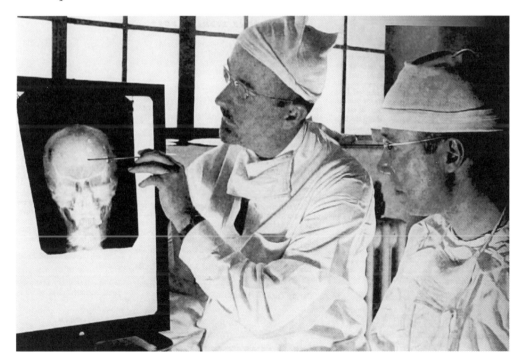

In the middle of the twentieth century, lobotomy, a surgical intervention in the brain, became a popular technique for treating the mentally ill.

Medicalisation

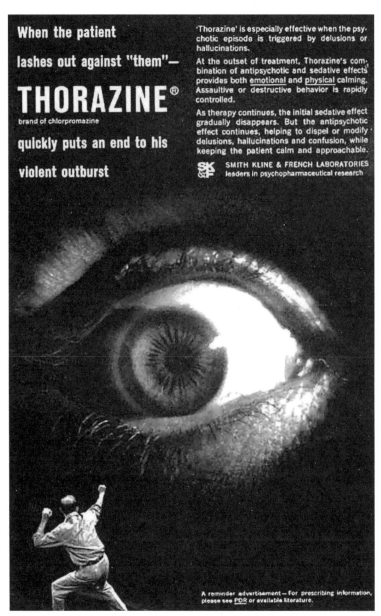

When the patient lashes out against "them"—

THORAZINE®
brand of chlorpromazine

quickly puts an end to his violent outburst

'Thorazine' is especially effective when the psychotic episode is triggered by delusions or hallucinations.

At the outset of treatment, Thorazine's combination of antipsychotic and sedative effects provides both _emotional_ and _physical_ calming. Assaultive or destructive behavior is rapidly controlled.

As therapy continues, the initial sedative effect gradually disappears. But the antipsychotic effect continues, helping to dispel or modify delusions, hallucinations and confusion, while keeping the patient calm and approachable.

SMITH KLINE & FRENCH LABORATORIES
leaders in psychopharmaceutical research

A reminder advertisement — For prescribing information, please see PDR or available literature.

Development of Drug Treatments

The development of drugs to treat symptoms rather than just control behaviour started in the 1950s. It was discovered that chlorpromazine, from a family of chemicals that had been used as dyes and as drugs to treat malaria and Parkinson's disease, also improved mood and induced, in some Parkinson's patients, euphoria. Chlorpromazine soon became the drug of choice to treat schizophrenia under the trade names Thorazine and Largactil and became very profitable for their manufacturers. This stimulated a search for other psychoactive drugs, with the result that more than 150 new medications for the treatment of mental disorders were developed between 1952 and 1975.

The number of people diagnosed with mental illness and receiving drug treatment has increased and is still increasing. In the US, outpatient visits that involved the prescription of medication only rose from 44 per cent to 57 per cent between 1998 and 2007. The increased medicalisation of mental illness is a contentious issue because drug treatment is expensive and its effectiveness is disputed. In 2011, the American Psychological Association began a campaign to increase the use of psychotherapy as an alternative to drug treatment.

PSYCHOLOGICAL APPROACHES TO MENTAL DISTRESS AND MENTAL HEALTH

We will now turn to distinctly psychological approaches to mental distress and mental health beginning with psychoanalysis and then look at psychotherapies, clinical psychology and the development of cognitive behavioural therapy (CBT).

Chlorpromazine, known under its trade name Thorazine, has become a very profitable drug for its manufacturers.

The Strange Case of Hysteria

In the nineteenth century the diagnosis of **hysteria** was common. This illness was seen as a woman's ailment; from the time of the ancient Greeks, it was thought to be caused by vapours from the womb or **hysterum** reaching the brain and causing disruption. At the Pitié-Salpêtrière Hospital in Paris, Jean-Martin Charcot (1825–93) broke the link between hysteria and sexual anatomy by diagnosing hysteria in men. Charcot believed that hysteria was the result of an unstable constitution that was also related to how easily a person could be hypnotised. Every week the great and good of Parisian high society could attend an open seminar where Charcot would explain his theories of hysteria and under hypnosis demonstrate the symptoms such as tetanus of the muscles and sensory insensitivity. Famously, Sigmund Freud visited Charcot in 1885 to learn about hysteria. Freud always kept a print of Brouillet's 'A Clinical Lesson at the Salpêtrière' by Pierre Aristide André Brouillet in his office.

Psychoanalysis

In the 1930s and 1940s, in both the United States and Europe, the dominant approach to psychopathology was *psychoanalysis*. This technique was created by Sigmund Freud (1856–1939) and developed largely outside of the university system in private practice. Freud, in contrast to Wundt (see Chapter 1), believed that psychology was not the scientific study of consciousness. He believed that conscious experience reflected just one part of the mind and that the mind also comprised a vast and not directly accessible *unconscious*.

Sigmund Freud created the technique of psychoanalysis, which examined the vast realm of the unconscious.

The id ('it')
The neonate's connection to the world is through the satisfaction of desire. The infant can suck or bite and is driven only by the pursuit of pleasure.

The ego ('I')
As the infant comes up against the outside world and learns through the process of potty training that other people exist, the sense of 'self' as separate from everyone else develops. The infant now distinguishes between fantasy and reality.

The superego ('above I')
At around eleven years old, the desire of the child for the opposite sex parent (*Oedipus conflict*) is resolved by taking – or 'introjecting' – the characteristics of the same sex parent. This introduces another 'voice' to the individual, which brings up the set of rules and taboos about right and wrong behaviour that came from the parent.

FREUD'S ACCOUNT OF THE STRUCTURE OF THE MIND AND ITS DEVELOPMENT

The ego is that part of the mind that is directly accessible. The pre-conscious is that part of memory that can be accessed at will. The unconscious realm of the *id* is not directly accessible because its desires might be too frightening for conscious experience and are kept repressed. Freud's diagram on page 194 indicates the relationship between *id*, *ego*, *superego* and perception (pcpt), pre-conscious and unconscious.

Freud's structural representation of the psyche (from New Introductory Lectures*).*

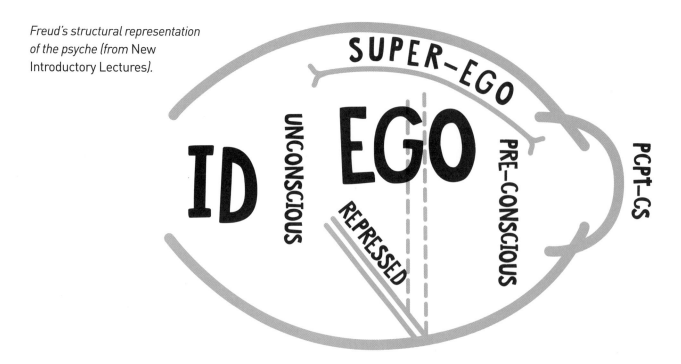

Carl Jung

Carl Jung (1875–1961) was trained as a psychiatrist working as an assistant to Eugen Bleuler. With Bleuler he studied 'dementia praecox' publishing a book of the same name in 1909. He observed that patients suffering from dementia praecox withdrew into themselves (introversion) whereas patients suffering from hysteria kept contact with others (extraverts). Jung briefly collaborated with Freud becoming the first president of the International Psychoanalytic Association but Freud broke with him after, Jung's 'Psychology of the Unconscious' presented the psyche as comprising of the conscious, personal unconscious and collective unconscious. Jung returned to his distinction between introversion and extraversion and argued that pairing them with sensation and intuition (irrational processes) and thinking and feeling (rational processes) producing eight personality **types**. This typology was used by **Katharine Cook Briggs** (1875–1968) to produce the **Myers–Briggs Type Indicator (MBTI)** (see page 227). The distinction between introversion and extraversion appears as a **dimension** in contemporary psychometric theories of personality.

Myers-Briggs Type Indicator

Psychoanalytic Treatment and Training

Psychoanalytic treatment is usually long term (over a year). In treatment, the analyst will use techniques such as dream analysis and free association to explore the patient's unconscious. Training as a psychoanalyst varies according to the particular school of analysis. Typically, it requires an intensive training analysis with sessions taking place five times a week over a period of four or five years. In addition to the training analysis, the prospective analyst conducts closely supervised psychoanalysis of two patients. Psychoanalysts are usually employed in private practice but there are some attached to the health service and universities. To undergo a full analysis is expensive. The fees depend on the analyst's experience and reputation. It is not uncommon for a fully analysis to cost more than £10,000 a year. Some psychoanalysts offer reduced rates for those on low wages, but these places are usually limited.

Carl Jung presented the psyche as divided between the conscious, personal unconscious and collective unconscious.

Freud's Case histories

Freud built his theory on the basis of a series of case studies rather than experiments or large scale surveys. One of the most famous case histories in psychoanalysis was carried out not by Freud himself but by his friend and colleague Josef Breuer. Breuer was treating a young woman who was referred to as Anna O. Anna was suffering from a variety of symptoms including that she was eating and drinking very little. Breuer got in the habit of visiting her each morning and talking to her while she was in a kind of dreamy, self-induced hypnotic state. In this state, she was able to talk about the onset of her symptoms that, when she was fully awake, she couldn't remember. When she remembered the onset of the symptoms they intensified and then subsided. Freud reasoned that the circumstances in which the symptoms first appeared were very painful and that these memories of trauma had been ***repressed***. The energy associated with this trauma was still there and was converted to physical symptoms. Bringing these unconscious memories to the conscious mind released the energy that had been damned up at the point of trauma and caused the physical symptoms to disappear. Breuer described Anna remembering that she has become afraid of drinking water when her dog-loving governess had allowed her pet to drink from a glass of water and then drank from the same glass. As a child, Anna could not comment on the event so her disgust and anger at the governess had been repressed.

Anna O is a key case study in the development of psychoanalysis because Freud deduced from her story the existence of unconscious behaviour, the mechanism of repression and the conversion of psychological trauma into physical symptoms.

Josef Breuer carried out the study of Anna O, which was a key moment in the development of psychoanalysis.

Psychotherapy

Classic psychoanalytic treatment is long term, time consuming and expensive. A patient might be in analysis for years, visiting the analyst for an hour each week. After Freud's death, psychoanalysis fragmented into different groups who emphasised or rejected different aspects of Freud's theories. These groups developed their own approaches to *psychotherapy* that drew on basic psychoanalytic insights, such as the importance of early childhood experience and the existence of repression. Often these *psychotherapeutic approaches* offered shorter and more specific problem-based therapy. It is beyond the scope of this chapter to describe all the different types of psychotherapy that developed after Freud. *Dryden's Handbook of Individual Therapy* provides a full list of these different psychotherapies, including those that take their starting point from Freud (such as Kleinian, Jungian and Adlerian) and those that had different foundations (such as *person centred therapy* and *rational emotive therapy*).

Psychotherapeutic approaches

Psychotherapy has fragmented into many different variants since Freud's original conception.

Types of Psychotherapy

Counselling

If *psychotherapy* might be regarded as a less intense version of psychoanalysis, then *counselling* might be considered a less intensive version of psychotherapy. Psychotherapists and counsellors share many techniques. While it is difficult to separate the two, in general, counselling is less about 'getting well' and removing symptoms and more about working out ways of living a more fulfilling life. As with psychoanalysis and psychotherapy, it is essential that the client seeks help rather than having treatment imposed on them by external forces, such as the family or general practitioner.

Transference — Psychoanalytically informed psychotherapists and counsellors share a number of key ideas. Among these is that in a therapeutic relationship the client, through a process of *transference*, projects characteristics of people they have had important relationships with onto the therapist and, in a sense, relives these relationships. During therapy, the therapist analyst will draw attention to the existence of *repression* and use techniques of *free association* and *dream analysis* in order to help the patient work through their *defence mechanisms* to understand their unconscious motives and desires.

Dream analysis

HUMANISTIC PSYCHOLOGY
According to Freud, the most we can expect from psychoanalysis is that *hysterical misery is transformed into common unhappiness.*

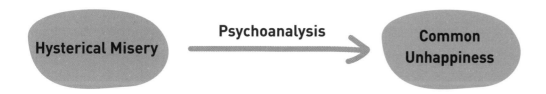

No doubt the removal of hysterical misery would be a great relief but in the 1940s some American psychologists became disillusioned with this pessimistic view of human nature. They were also disillusioned with psychology, more generally believing that the determinism of the learning theories of Pavlov and Skinner robbed people of their freedom and individuality (see Chapter 2). Carl Rogers (1902–87) and Abraham Maslow (1908–70) were together instrumental in orchestrating what they called a 'third' force in psychology that would work to increase our natural capacity for growth and creativity.

The major therapies associated with this *third force* are person-centred or client-centred therapy and Gestalt therapy. These therapies share central assumptions about human nature. They are described as humanistic because they address the human as a complete person rather than as a collection of associations or unconscious desires. One of the key differences between these humanistic approaches and psychoanalytically informed psychotherapies

Third force

is the role of the therapist, who is not neutral. Instead, the therapist affirms and encourages the client and has an attitude of positive regard. The documentary *Three Approaches to Psychotherapy I, II, and III* was released in 1965 and shows a woman called Gloria in therapy with three different therapists: Albert Ellis, Carl Rogers, and Frederick (Fritz) Perls. To understand how the postulates of humanistic psychology are implemented there is no better way than watching this film, which is readily available on-line.

NAMES TO KNOW: HUMANISTIC PSYCHOLOGISTS

Carl Rogers (1902–87)

Abraham Maslow (1908–70)

The Five Postulates of Humanistic Psychology

1 Human beings, as human, supersede the sum of their parts. They cannot be reduced to components.
2 Human beings have their existence in a uniquely human context, as well as in a cosmic ecology.
3 Human beings are aware and aware of being aware – i.e., they are conscious. Human consciousness always includes an awareness of oneself in the context of other people.
4 Human beings have some choice and, with that, responsibility.
5 Human beings are intentional, aim at goals, are aware that they cause future events, and seek meaning, value and creativity.
– 'The Five Basic Postulates of Humanistic Psychology', *Journal of Humanistic Psychology* 2006; 46; 239

THE ROLE OF THE CLINICAL PSYCHOLOGIST

At first, psychiatrists and psychoanalysts/psychotherapists had limited interactions with academic psychology. This began to change after World War II when veterans began to return home from serving abroad. These veterans were not only in need of psychological help to adjust to civilian life but, for many, also to get help with the trauma they had experienced on the battlefield. The Veterans Association in the USA funded the training of psychologists who would have the clinical methods to deal with these problems. The courses that were funded were many and varied.

The Veterans Association in the United States has sponsored the training of psychologists to help veterans return to civilian life.

In 1949, after intense consultation with academics and therapists, the Boulder Conference on Graduate Education in Clinical Psychology laid out a *standard curriculum* combining research skills and clinical practice. The Boulder model is one of scientist/practitioner; the professional clinical psychologist will apply interventions based on current psychological research and systematically feed the outcomes of their practice back into basic research. The goal of this scientist/practitioner model is to produce a virtuous circle in which good therapy informs research, which then produces better therapy and so on.

Clinical Psychology in the UK and the Development of Behavioural Therapy

Hans Eysenck (see Chapter 8) visited the USA in the late 1940s to learn about the new approaches being developed to train clinical psychologists. He was impressed by the Boulder model and on his return to the UK he set up the first British training course in Clinical Psychology. Eysenck's background was in the study of individual differences and learning theory. He had no time for psychoanalysis or psychodynamically informed therapy, both popular in America, and so designed his own curriculum based on psychometric research and Pavlov's classical conditioning.

Eysenck worked with *Joseph Wolpe* (1915–97) to develop *behavioural therapy*. The best-known and most effective approach they developed was *desensitisation therapy* for the treatment of phobias. These behavioural therapies were designed to change behaviour and were explicitly goal orientated. If the problematic behaviour was removed then the case was closed.

Desensitisation therapy

BEHAVIOURAL THERAPY ▶ *a range of techniques designed to change behaviour, based on the principles of classical and operant conditioning.*

Systematic Desensitization

Wolpe had been inducing artificial neuroses in animals. He then tackled the problem of removing these neuroses. Through this research, he developed a treatment programme for use with humans that he called *systematic desensitisation*. He set up a hierarchy of anxiety-provoking situations and then got clients to learn to cope with each level of anxiety using relaxation techniques, steadily moving through the hierarchy. This could be done using the imagination or in reality. For example, to treat someone who is scared of flying, each of the steps necessary to complete a journey by air would be tackled in turn. The client would first be taught relaxation techniques, such as controlled breathing, and then establish a hierarchy of fear (see figure below). They would then work through each of the steps of the hierarchy, pairing the actual behaviour (or visualising the behaviour) with the relaxation techniques. Once the client was comfortable with one step in the hierarchy they moved up to the next step.

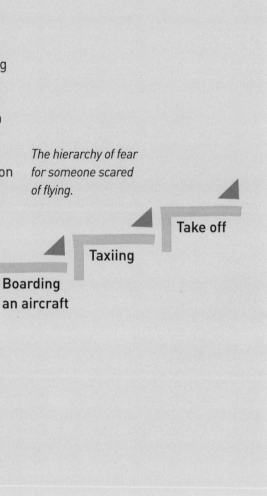

The hierarchy of fear for someone scared of flying.

Take off

Taxiing

Boarding an aircraft

Buying a ticket for a flight

Visiting an airport

Checking in at the airport

Simulated flight in a simulator

Entering a flight simulator

COGNITIVE BEHAVIOURAL THERAPY

Wolpe and Eysenck built clinical psychology in the UK on the foundations of behavioural therapy. It worked well for the treatment of phobias and some anxiety disorders, but for the treatment of depression results were poor. In the US, psychoanalytically informed therapists were finding that they too were having limited success in treating depression.

Albert Ellis and Aaron Beck

Two of these therapists were Albert Ellis and Aaron Beck; their work rejected psychoanalytic concepts. They married the behavioural therapies advocated by Eysenck and Wolpe with a new emphasis on thinking and with problems of thinking.

Albert Ellis (1913–2007) found that, when he was conducting psychoanalytic therapy, rather than reliving episodes of their early childhoods, his patients seemed to be in the grip of faulty thinking that they could not shake off. Instead of spending more and more time trying to probe the unconscious, Ellis decided to tackle the faulty thinking directly. The documentary *Three Approaches to Psychotherapy I, II, and III*, mentioned earlier, shows Ellis conducting a therapeutic session.

Rational emotive therapy

Ellis called his new approach **Rational Emotive Therapy** (RET) and later added the term behavioural to the title to give **Rational Emotive Behavioural Therapy** (REBT) to stress the importance of the link between feelings, thoughts and behaviour that was central to his theorising.

> **NAMES TO KNOW: COGNITIVE BEHAVIOURAL THERAPISTS**
>
> **Albert Ellis** (1913–2007)
>
> **Aaron Beck** (1921–present)

> **RATIONAL EMOTIVE BEHAVIOURAL THERAPY ▶**
> stresses the links between feelings, thoughts and behaviour.

Aaron Beck rejected the psychoanalytic approach and instead built on the behavioural therapies of Eysenck and Wolpe.

Albert Ellis and the ABC Model of Human Behaviour

Ellis argued that human distress is not so much about what the world does to us but how we think about the world and deal with those thoughts. This is expressed in his *ABC Model*, which shows how an *Activating event elicits* our *Beliefs* about the world and has *Consequences* for the way we act or feel.

Types of Psychotherapy

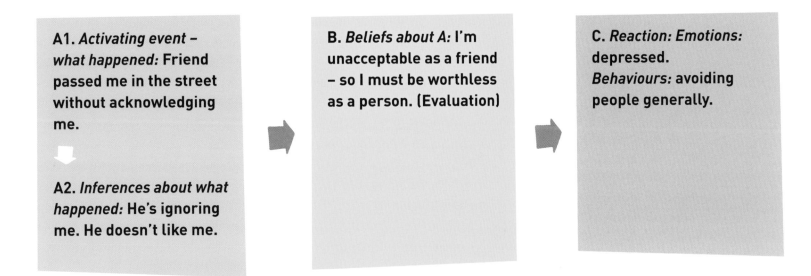

A1. *Activating event – what happened:* Friend passed me in the street without acknowledging me.

A2. *Inferences about what happened:* He's ignoring me. He doesn't like me.

B. *Beliefs about A:* I'm unacceptable as a friend – so I must be worthless as a person. (Evaluation)

C. *Reaction: Emotions:* depressed. *Behaviours:* avoiding people generally.

– Wayne Froggatt, 'A Brief Introduction to Rational Emotive Behavioural Therapy', https://www.rational.org.nz/prof-docs/Intro-REBT.pdf

One of the key goals of Ellis' approach to therapy is to help clients identify their beliefs. The *Consequences* (how we feel and behave) are usually clear to us, but the *Beliefs* that drive these behaviours and feelings are often harder to recognise. In therapy these beliefs can be uncovered, and the basis for those beliefs challenged, leading to their replacement with more realistic or appropriate understanding.

Aaron Beck (1921–present) was coming to similar to conclusions to Ellis. In therapy sessions, he came to believe that the reactions of his clients were not structured by the unconscious and processes of repression but were clinging to unhelpful beliefs. He found that his depressed clients were plagued by an internal dialogue of automatic negative thoughts that undermined their ability to act. Anxious clients were tormented by beliefs that the world was inherently terrifying and they were always just one step away from disaster. Beck worked with his patients to challenge these dysfunctional beliefs and replace them with a more realistic view of the world that acknowledges that bad things do happen but that it is not necessary to exaggerate or catastrophise them.

Beck's cognitive triad – his account of the vicious circle that must be broken to recover from depression. This illustration shows how negative views of oneself, the world and the future are interrelated.

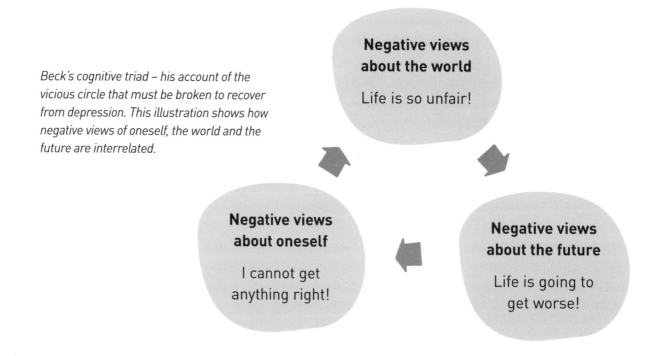

Negative views about the world

Life is so unfair!

Negative views about oneself

I cannot get anything right!

Negative views about the future

Life is going to get worse!

Key Features of Cognitive Behavioural Therapy

The distinctive features of CBT are that the therapist and the client actively work together on clearly specified problems. The focus is on the present, unlike psychoanalytically informed therapy. The client learns how to work on their own problems and, in effect, becomes their own therapist able to recognise biases in their own thinking. They are then armed with a set of skills and techniques that they can use on themselves without supervision.

The Role of Cognitive Behavioural Therapy Today

Cognitive behavioural therapy has evolved since the early work of Ellis and Beck. Originally a treatment for depression, the UK National Institute of Clinical Excellence (NICE) recommends CBT for the treatment of anxiety disorders and bipolar disorder; its use for the treatment of psychosis is currently being evaluated. The National Health Service (NHS) uses CBT for treating obsessive-compulsive disorders, panic disorders, post-traumatic stress disorder, phobias, eating disorders and as a way for people with irritable bowel syndrome and chronic fatigue syndrome to better deal with their symptoms. CBT is delivered by clinical psychologists and trained CBT therapists. The Royal College of Psychiatrists endorses self-help and online CBT and there are apps based on CBT principles see https://overcoming.co.uk.

Becoming a Clinical Psychologist

Many undergraduate psychology students start their degrees with the intention of becoming clinical psychologists because they have a desire to help other people overcome psychological distress. The field is very rewarding but also very challenging. To qualify as a clinical psychologist it is necessary to complete a professional doctorate and competition is stiff to get on to these courses. It is advisable to seek experience working as a volunteer to gain relevant experience and to help decide if the field really is for you.

CLINICAL PSYCHOLOGY

The history of clinical psychology is intimately linked with the history of psychiatry and psychoanalysis. For centuries, strange or abnormal behaviour was characterised in Western Europe as being the result of witchcraft or evil spirits. A shift to a more compassionate understanding of 'madness' occurred in the eighteenth century, when reformers such as William Tuke (1732–1822) founded institutions like the York Retreat in 1796 to offer 'moral treatment', combining gentle care with rehabilitation. In the nineteenth century, psychiatry developed as a medical specialisation. The medical understanding of 'madness' as being the result of underlying physical brain abnormalities was crude. Early psychiatrists distinguished between *psychoses* and *neuroses*, with psychoses referring to behavioural and cognitive symptoms and neuroses to their neurological causes. But this distinction was soon blurred, with the difference being understood in terms of the severity of symptoms rather than as cause and effect. Emil Kraepelin (1856–1926) distinguished between *dementia praecox* and *manic depression*, classifications that were then revised by Eugen Bleuler (1857–1939). In 1908, he coined the term '*schizophrenia*' to replace dementia praecox. The medical model developed over the 20th century. In the 1950s, *antipsychotic* drugs such as chlorpromazine (trade names Thorazine and Largactil) went on the market. In the 1980s, the *selective serotonin reuptake inhibitors* (SSRIs), such as fluoxetine (tradename Prozac), became the psychiatric treatment of choice for depression. The tradition of 'talking cures' began with Sigmund Freud's (1856–1939) treatment of hysteria and other neuroses, using his method of psychoanalysis. In the twentieth century, a wide range of psychotherapies were developed that drew on at least some of Freud's key concepts, such as the unconscious or repression. In the 1960s, a new family of therapies was developed that drew on learning theory and ideas about the self-regulation of thoughts. These developed into cognitive behavioural therapy (CBT), which is currently the non-chemical treatment of choice for depression and anxiety.

Institutions like the York Retreat in the north of England, founded in 1796, offered a more compassionate approach to the mentally ill than the accusations of witchcraft that preceded them.

The Scientist Practitioner Model – Health
Psychology – Forensic Psychology –
Educational Psychology – Occupational
Psychology – Sports Psychology

MISINFORMATION EFFECT

HUMAN ASPECTS OF ILLNESS

HEALTH BELIEF MODEL

EYEWITNESS TESTIMONY

MEMORY

CHANGING BEHAVIOURS

HEALTH PSYCHOLOGY

SCIENTIST PRACTITIONER MODEL

FORENSIC PSYCHOLOGY

SOCIAL FACILITATION

EXERCISE PSYCHOLOGISTS

COLEMAN GRIFFITH

ASSESSING WELLBEING

PROFESSIONAL PSYCHOLOGY

SPORTS PSYCHOLOGY

ELITE PERFORMANCE

LEARNING DIFFICULTIES

EDUCATIONAL PSYCHOLOGY

OCCUPATIONAL PSYCHOLOGY

MOTIVATION

VISUALISATION

INFLUENCE OF TEACHERS

SCIENTIFIC MANAGEMENT

HAWTHORNE STUDIES

ROBERT ROSENTHAL

WORKER BEHAVIOUR

PREPARATION FOR THE WORKPLACE

Students who graduate with a degree in psychology have writing skills, research skills and data analysis skills that can be used in many different fields of work unrelated to psychology, including business, advertising, teaching and human resources. In the UK, around 10 per cent of psychology graduates remain in education taking PhDs in order to become academic psychologists, or professional doctorates to qualify in one of the seven titles protected by law that can only be used by chartered psychologists.

Although there are some differences between the US and UK systems, there is much overlap. Professional recognition or certification may also differ in other countries around the world but, again, will be broadly similar. Professional psychologists who move to a country with a different certification system must apply to the relevant regulatory body for recognition of their qualifications. In this chapter, we examine the professional areas recognised in the UK. Most degree courses cover these areas in the curriculum to introduce students to potential career options. *Career options* (Clinical psychology and counselling psychology were dealt with in the last chapter and so will not be included here.)

BRITISH PSYCHOLOGICAL SOCIETY PROFESSIONAL AREAS	AMERICAN BOARD OF PROFESSIONAL PSYCHOLOGY
Clinical Psychologists	Behavioural and Cognitive
Counselling Psychologists	Clinical Child and Adolescent
Educational Psychologists	Clinical Health
Forensic Psychologists	Clinical
Health Psychologists	Clinical Neuropsychology
Occupational Psychologists	Clinical Child Psychology
Sport and Exercise Psychologists	Counseling Psychology
	Couple and Family
	Forensic Psychology
	Geropsychology
	Group
	Organisational and Business Consulting
	Police and Public Safety Psychology
	Rehabilitation
	School
	Psychoanalysis

PROFESSIONAL PSYCHOLOGY AND THE SCIENTIST PRACTITIONER MODEL

Professional areas of psychology share the scientist practitioner model described in the previous chapter (Clinical Psychology). In this model, practice and research go hand in hand and inform each other.

Students studying professional doctorates gain subject-specific knowledge and learn advanced research methods, which enable them to evaluate their own practices and critically assess new research findings. As professionals, they will also be expected to develop professional skills so they can follow ethical and legal standards and learn the skills that prepare them for managing projects and teams.

Professional psychologists follow the scientist-practitioner model, just as clinical psychologists do.

HEALTH PSYCHOLOGY

Background and Context

The medical model described in the previous chapter in the context of mental illness conceptualises disease as the result of physiological or physical disorders that lead to abnormal functioning. The body is conceived as a very complex machine that can be 'fixed' with appropriate interventions. Sometimes the interventions have unintended side effects that might affect the functioning of other bodily systems. Sometimes the technology available to the medical profession cannot 'fix' the problem and the patient stops functioning and dies.

The medical model has been incredibly successful, as indexed by the increases in life expectancy and survival rates from illness that within living memory were very poor. Our doctors are well versed in the medical model but they do not regard us simply as machines to be fixed. Increasingly, they are being trained to recognise that humans have feelings and might be scared or experience great suffering. Health psychologists appreciate the technological sophistication of the medical model but are also concerned with these *human aspects* of experiencing illness.

Drawing on psychological theories, health psychologists systematically and empirically investigate the *psychological* and *social* aspects of illness and work to enhance health and wellbeing and not just to increase survival. These psychological and social aspects of illness are now especially important as our populations get older and many more people and their families have to negotiate old age. An ageing population also means that more people are living with chronic illnesses for extended periods of time.

Health psychologists help to address the issues caused by 'lifestyle' choices such as smoking.

We are also dealing with a population that suffers from diseases that are the result of so called 'lifestyle' choices, such as overeating, smoking, drug misuse, unprotected sex and excess alcohol consumption, and not just infections and injuries. Health psychologists address these issues by conducting basic research in departments of psychology but they can also be found in departments of nutrition, health sciences and medicine. They also work with local authorities and public health departments. Some health psychologists work directly with patients and clients in health care settings such as hospitals and general practices. Health psychologists often work in multi-disciplinary teams made up of other professionals including nurses, dieticians, surgeons and rehabilitation therapists. We will now examine some of the areas in which health psychologists contribute to enhancing health.

Health Psychologists work as part of a team including nurses, dieticians, surgeons and rehabilitation therapists.

Assessing Health and Wellbeing
Using psychometric methods to design reliable and valid measures of health and wellbeing.

Stress
Investigating the role of stress as a trigger of illness and the evaluation of coping strategies designed to reduce it.

Investigating Health Inequalities
Investigating the effects of social class, gender and ethnicity on access to health care and subsequent treatment.

ELEMENTS OF HEALTH PSYCHOLOGY

Encouraging Health Enhancing Behaviours
Researching how adopting nutritious diets, and taking part in regular exercise programmes and community activities can actively promote good health. Currently, health psychologists are examining how practices such as yoga and mindfulness can improve both mental and physical health. Much work is also carried out to increase the rates of uptake of the preventative services provided by the health service, such as screening for breast cancer, bowel cancer and so forth. An important area of research is into finding ways to encourage people to adhere to their prescribed treatments. The *health belief model* is used extensively by health psychologists to understand why some people engage in risky behaviours and others engage in health-enhancing behaviours.

Identifying and Addressing Risky Behaviours
Working with epidemiologists and medical professionals to identify behaviours that result in disease. Health psychologists conduct research on, for example, behaviours that lead to obesity, alcohol abuse, smoking and unprotected sex.

Health psychologists are now examining how activities like yoga can improve mental and physical health.

EXAMPLE OF HEALTH PSYCHOLOGY IN ACTION

Health Belief Model

While working in the USA health services during the 1950s, social psychologists Godfrey Hochbaum (1916–99), Irwin Rosenstock (1925–2001)and Stephen Kegels (1945–present) became increasingly concerned about the failure of a screening programme to identify people suffering from the early stages of tuberculosis. The programme involved taking mobile X-ray equipment directly into communities yet very few people asked to be tested. Drawing on the social psychology of attitudes, Hochbaum and his colleagues developed the *health belief model* (HBM) in order to understand why people were not engaging with the screening programme. They discovered that the difference between those who wanted to be tested and those that did not was related to whether or not they believed they were at risk and how seriously they evaluated that risk. The basic module has been refined and elaborated on over the years but is still widely used to understand potential barriers to changes in health behaviours.

EXAMPLE OF HEALTH BELIEF MODEL

This table shows how the HBM can be used to design programmes to increase the rate of use of condoms by young people.

1. Perceived Susceptibility
Believe they could get pregnant or infected with a sexually transmitted disease (STD).

2. Perceived Severity
Believe that the consequences of pregnancy or STD are serious.

3. Perceived Benefits
Believe that condoms prevent pregnancy and STDs.

4. Perceived Barriers
Identification of personal barriers:
decreased sexual enjoyment,
embarrassment and so forth.

5. Cues to Action
Reminders that condoms are available.

6. Self-Efficacy
Believing that they can use a condom correctly.

FORENSIC PSYCHOLOGY

Background and Context

Forensic psychologists prepare reports and other material for use as evidence in court or as an aid to the criminal justice system. They work in the prison service, offender rehabilitation units, secure hospitals and with social services. They conduct academic research and work with offenders, police officers, security services and the general public.

Forensic Psychology was one of the first applied areas of psychology to be developed. Hugo Münsterberg (1863–1916) in the first decade of the 20th century published *On the Witness Stand* (Münsterberg, 1908), in which he described how psychological factors impact how crimes are investigated and prosecuted. He warned against the coercive interrogation of suspects and the problems of eyewitness testimony which prefigured much of contemporary research in forensic psychology.

Today, forensic psychologists apply psychological theories drawn from social psychology, individual differences and cognitive psychology to conduct research on interviewing witnesses and suspects. They may be required to give evidence in court as expert witnesses and may be asked to give advice to parole boards on the risk of reoffending. They also look at the special issues raised when interviewing witnesses and suspects who come from vulnerable groups. They investigate how juries come to decisions and work on programmes to reduce reoffending. They may work directly with offenders to design programmes to reduce reoffending or at the institutional level to reduce stress for both staff and prisoners.

NAMES TO KNOW: HEALTH BELIEF MODEL

Godfrey Hochbaum (1916–99)

Irwin Rosenstock (1925–2001)

Stephen Kegels (1945–present)

Working with witnesses

FORENSIC PSYCHOLOGY ▶ *preparing reports and other material for use as evidence in the criminal justice system.*

Elizabeth Loftus, a forensic psychologist, has repeatedly been called as an expert witness to help resolve disputes about eyewitness testimony.

FORENSIC PSYCHOLOGY IN ACTION: EYEWITNESS TESTIMONY

One of the most contentious issues in forensic psychology is the evaluation of eyewitness testimony. We have already learned (Chapter 3: Cognitive Psychology) that Frederick Bartlett thought of remembering as a constructive process, rather than something that is fixed in time. In a court setting, eyewitnesses are asked about their certainty in recognising people and recalling events that actually occurred. Accuracy of recall is paramount as someone's life and liberty may be at stake. Yet Elizabeth F. Loftus (1944– present), an experimental cognitive psychologist and forensic psychologist, has been called as an expert witness in numerous cases of disputed eyewitness testimony. Her research has found that witnesses are often *certain* about events that have *not* occurred.

Loftus took as her starting point an experimental protocol called the Deese/Roediger–McDermott paradigm. In this protocol, participants are presented with lists of words and asked to memorise them. They are then given a recognition task that includes 'lure' words that were not in the initial lists but are closely associated with those words. When presented with a recognition task that includes the 'lure' words, participants are usually convinced they saw them in the initial list.

Words semantically related to the non-presented lure word 'sweet'.

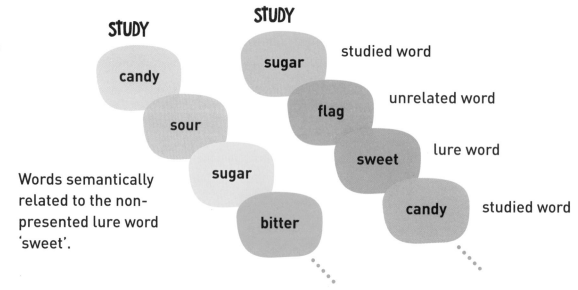

A schematic representation of the Deese/Roediger–McDermott (DRM) paradigm. From Budson et al (2002). 'Suppression of false recognition in Alzheimer's disease and in patients with frontal lobe lesions'. Brain, Volume 125, Issue 12. Pages 2750–65.

MISINFORMATION EFFECT ▶ *false memory of an event as a consequence of being given misleading information after the event.*

Loftus and Palmer demonstrated that this *misinformation* effect occurs when misleading information is provided to witnesses after an event, but prior to having their memory tested. In an experiment that has become highly influential, Loftus and Palmer showed participants a short film in which two cars collide. The experimental manipulation was to ask the participants how fast the cars were going before they smashed/collided with/bumped/hit/contacted each other?

Loftus and Palmer asked the participants in their study how fast the cars were going after watching a short film of a car crash. They found that changing the verb used to describe the incident resulted in different estimates of the speed of the vehicles.

As the verb used to describe the interaction between the two cars becomes more active, so the participants' estimate of the speed the cars were travelling increases. When the participants were asked if they had seen any broken glass (no broken glass was shown in the film), those who were asked about the car 'smash' were more likely to claim they had seen broken glass. The implication of this research for the criminal justice system is that interviewers must take care when questioning witnesses so they do not cause unconscious bias or distortion in the answers. Eyewitness testimony is still a very active area of forensic psychology.

Results of a Study into the Misinformation Effect

When participants were asked to estimate the speed of cars involved in the accident.

Verb	Estimated Speed (mph)
Smashed	40.8
Collided	39.3
Bumped	38.1
Hit	34.0
Contacted	31.8

When participants were asked if they had seen any broken glass

Response	Yes	No
Smashed	16	34
Hit	7	43
Control	6	44

Loftus, E. and Palmer, J. (1974). 'Reconstruction of automobile destruction: An example of the interaction between language and memory'. *Journal of Verbal Learning and Verbal Behavior*, 13(5), pp.585–589.

Background and Context

Psychologists have long had a close connection with education. The behaviourists put learning at the heart of psychology and B.F. Skinner developed so called 'teaching machines' based on the principles of *operant conditioning*, which he proposed as a replacement for traditional classroom learning (see page 28). Each child sat in front of a machine and proceeded through a curriculum

Educational psychologists help to develop new teaching techniques, identify learning disabilities and advise teachers on how to work with students with emotional problems.

split up into its smallest elements. He or she could not proceed to the next element until the current element was understood. Learning was at the pace of the individual child and, since the elements were small and built on each other, the child was more likely to experience success.

Piaget's *genetic epistemology* (see page 95) was very different, requiring the child to be engaged in activity in order to learn. Vygotsky went on to argue that learning did not take place in isolation and required social interaction. The development of cognitive psychology (see Chapter 3) has impacted on education through the development of models of reading based on information processing principles. Educational psychologists have, therefore, a rich psychological research base to draw on to help children and young people in school and college settings.

Role of the Educational Psychologist

Educational psychologists work with children and young people in education, including in early year settings, schools, colleges, nurseries and pupil referral units. They are employed by local authorities and also independent schools. Many more educational psychologists now work in private practice. The educational psychologist works with individual pupils/students, teachers and parents. They may also be involved in developing policy and the design and organisation of education services.

Educational psychologists may be asked to assess learning difficulties and developmental disorders. They may also investigate and advise on social and emotional problems and work with schools to develop strategies to help children with disabilities integrate into mainstream schools. They may be involved in the training of teachers and learning-support assistants. The main tools of the educational psychologist are classroom observations, interviews and assessments. A typical educational support assessment would start with a meeting with teachers and parents to discuss their concerns, followed by classroom and playground observations. This might be followed up with standardised assessments such as IQ tests and tools designed to assess emotional development.

Educational Psychology in Action

The influence of teachers was demonstrated by the psychologist Robert Rosenthal (1933–present), working with elementary school principal Lenore Jacobson. Rosenthal had been studying the effect of experimenter expectations on the performance of rats running mazes. He found that when experimenters were given rats that had been labelled 'bright', the animals ran mazes faster than those rats that had been labelled 'dull'. This kind of experimenter expectancy effect has consequences for how we run experiments and suggests that expectancies must be carefully controlled.

In 1963, Rosenthal moved out of the laboratory and into the classroom, working in a California elementary school. He tested all the students and then told the teachers that about 20 per cent of the students were 'intellectual bloomers' and would show marked cognitive improvement over the coming year. This was a lie; the 'intellectual bloomers' were picked at random. The pupils who had been labelled 'intellectual bloomers' gained significantly more over the year than the other students. This shows that teacher expectations have a great effect on the performance of children and more generally highlights the problem of 'labelling'. Rosenthal and Jacobson published a book-length account of this study in 1968 with the title *Pygmalion in the Classroom: Teacher Expectation and Pupils' Intellectual Development.*

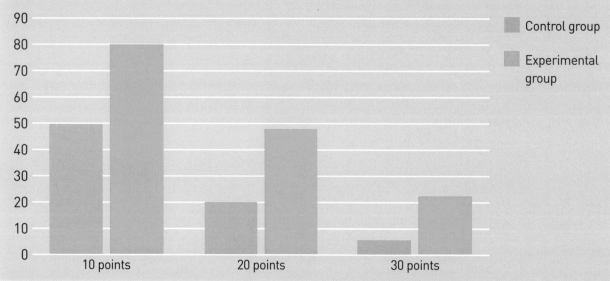

Bar chart shows the percentage IQ gain of students over an academic year. Rosenthal, R., &. Jacobson, L. (1963). 'Teachers' expectancies: Determinants of pupils' IQ gains'. Psychological Reports, 19, 115-118.

OCCUPATIONAL PSYCHOLOGY

Background and Context

Occupational psychology (or industrial psychology, as it is known in the US) uses psychological theories and approaches to enhance effectiveness in the work place.

At the turn of the twemtieth century, Frederick Taylor (1856–1915) invented ***scientific management*** (also called 'Taylorism'). The goal of scientific management was the maximisation of output and profit. Each task in a factory was to be carefully broken down into a series of simple mechanical steps. Workers were selected on the basis of who could complete those tasks, and then closely supervised and evaluated. The psychologist Hugo Münsterberg (1863–1916) was sympathetic to scientific management and advocated the use of psychometric tools to guide employee selection. He also advocated the provision of vocational guidance to help young people understand their own capacities and interests. In 1913 he published *Psychology and Industrial Efficiency*.

> **NAMES TO KNOW:**
> **OCCUPATIONAL PSYCHOLOGY**
>
> *Frederick Taylor* (1856–1915)
>
> *Hugo Münsterberg* (1863–1916)
>
> *Elton Mayo* (1880–1949)

Hugo Münsterberg suggested using psychometric tools to make employment decisions.

223

At Western Electric's Hawthorne Works, near Chicago, Elton Mayo ran a series of psychological experiments in the 1920s and 1930s.

It is against this background that Elton Mayo (1880–1949) got involved in a series of experiments being run at Western Electric's Hawthorne works, just outside Chicago. Starting in 1928, these experiments ran for more than 10 years and demonstrated some of the limits of scientific management. In particular, they demonstrated that when workers were given more rather

than less control over their work environment and allowed to set their own standards for output, absenteeism fell and production increased. The Hawthorne studies showed that worker participation and job satisfaction were more important than physical working conditions and set the scene for studying the psychological and social aspects of work.

Occupational/Industrial Psychology in Action: The Hawthorne Studies

The aim of the Hawthorne studies initially was to investigate the effects of the physical work environment on worker performance. Two groups of assembly workers at the factory were taken from the general work population to be part of the study. First, the level of lighting was increased, which resulted in increased production. Further increases in the level of lighting also increased production. Surprisingly, reversion to the initial level of lighting and even reducing the level of lighting to *below* that level also increased production.

Relay Assembly Test Room Experiments
To further investigate this unexpected result, another series of experiments was designed that manipulated other variables, including the provision of rest periods and financial incentives. Overall, each change resulted in increased output. When conditions were returned to those in place before the experiment began, productivity was at its highest ever level.

Bank Wiring Room Studies
In a further set of experiments, workers were employed to wire, solder and inspect electronic devices. Again, the provision of rest periods and financial incentives were manipulated but this time production remained constant no matter what incentives were offered. The workers actively discouraged each other from increasing their work rates.

Understanding Worker Behaviour
Mayo identified the different styles of supervision as the cause of the difference between the illumination and relay assembly test studies and the bank wiring room study. In the first two studies, the lead psychologist encouraged the workers and took them into his trust. In the bank wiring room study, however, the psychologist kept his distance and acted as an objective observer. This resulted in the workers forming an informal group with its own standards rather than forming a group that included the psychologists and managers, as in the first two studies.

Where do you find Occupational/Industrial Psychologists?
Human resource departments within large companies often employ occupational psychologists full time. Smaller companies are more likely to employ occupational psychologists as consultants. They also work in government departments and pursue basic research in academic settings. Specialist psychometric publishing companies employ occupational psychologists to develop new tests and to train others in the use of these tests.

Psychological Assessment

Psychological assessment is a multi-million dollar business. For example, one of the most widely known assessment tools is the Myers–Briggs personality test. This retails for $15 to $40 and is taken by around two million people every year. *The Washington Post* estimates that this test, and other tests and guides associated with it, are worth over $20 million a year to its publishers.

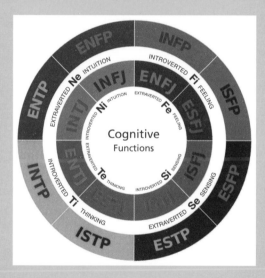

The Myers-Briggs personality test is one of the most popular psychological assessments available today.

AREAS IN OCCUPATIONAL PSYCHOLOGY

Wellbeing at Work

Work place stress and absenteeism costs industry millions of pounds a year in lost production. Occupational psychologists work to develop the wellbeing of their workforce in order to increase resilience and health. They also design interventions and policies to address bullying and harassment.

Work Design and Development

Occupational psychologists can help the workforce adjust to organisational change and design structures that maximise communication within the workplace.

Leadership, Motivation and Engagement

Occupational therapists are involved in teaching leadership skills and helping managers understand the psychology of motivation and engage with the workforce.

Learning, Training and Development

Drawing on the psychology of motivation and life span development, occupational psychologists advise staff on professional development.

Coleman Griffith brought sports psychology to baseball. Unfortunately for the Chicago Cubs, his advice did not result in immediate success.

NAMES TO KNOW: SPORTS PSYCHOLOGY

Coleman Griffith (1893–1966)

Norman Triplett (1861–1934)

SPORTS PSYCHOLOGY

Background and Context

In the 1920s, Coleman Griffith (1893–1966) opened a sports research laboratory at the University of Illinois. He published research on training methods for American football and basketball stating:

'When an athlete goes out on the field for a contest he does not leave his mind tucked away in a locker with his shoes, his watch and his hat'.

Griffith's Illinois laboratory closed in 1935. In 1938, Griffith was employed by the owner of the Chicago Cubs baseball team to improve player performance. He brought in a slow-motion film camera to record batting and pitching practice and advised the management to spend more time training players in conditions that were similar to match condition. His time at the Cubs was fraught with problems and he was in continual conflict with the coach. The Cubs did not perform well and Griffith was sacked. Nonetheless, Griffith's failures did not prevent more teams from turning to professional psychologists to gain an edge. From the 1930s to the 1990s sports psychology did, at least in the English-speaking world, take off.

*Growth of sports
psychology*

*Exercise and
wellbeing*

Elite and Non-elite Sport and Exercise

By the end of the twentieth century, the introduction of satellite and cable television had vastly increased the revenue of professional sports and these rewards have continued to grow. As a consequence, more and more sports have moved from amateur to professional status. Physical conditioning and nutrition have also improved, making the margin between success and failure very small.

Athletes and administrators who searched for small improvements in performance that could bridge the gap between success and failure turned to psychology as one approach. This led to a dramatic increase in the application of sports psychology and the professionalisation of the area.

This has gone hand in hand with increased research into the benefits of behaviours that enhance health in the general population. This research has shown that regular exercise can protect individuals from physical diseases and can also enhance wellbeing. Sport and exercise is increasingly recommended across a person's lifespan, with the benefits for maintaining good health into old age being particularly marked.

Exercise has been found to be one of the cheapest and most effective ways of improving health and wellbeing, opening up a new market for experts in the psychology of exercise. Today, sports and exercise psychologists work in a range of settings including full-time posts and consultancy work with professional sports teams and national governing bodies. Exercise psychologists may also work in private practice and with health teams working in hospitals and prisons. The increased use of sports and exercise as a means of enhancing wellbeing is leading to more and more overlap between sports psychology and health psychology.

Psychology of Elite Performance
Elite athletes and other sports men and women require months or years of physical training in preparation for an event that might take only seconds or minutes. Sports psychologists help them by, for example, setting goals and dealing with the day-to-day grind of training as well as the psychological aspects of injuries that may prevent athletes from taking part in training and competition.

Motivation and Maintenance of Exercise Behaviour
Exercise psychologists draw on the techniques of health psychology and counselling psychology to help people take up exercise after illness.

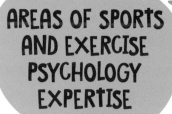

AREAS OF SPORTS AND EXERCISE PSYCHOLOGY EXPERTISE

Individual and Group Processes
Sports psychologists advise managers and trainers on group dynamics in order to maintain and enhance team morale.

Sport, Exercise and Mental Health
Sports psychologists work with health psychologists and other mental health professionals to develop exercise interventions to help clients deal with depression and anxiety.

Motor Skill Acquisition and Performance
Sports psychologists use visualisation techniques and behavioural psychology to guide skill acquisition and habitual performance.

Sports Psychology in Action

In 1898, Norman Triplett (1861–1934) carried out what is arguably the first experiment in social psychology and in sports psychology. Triplett was a keen amateur cyclist and member of a cycling association called the League of American Wheelmen. Having spent time examining race records, he noticed that race times differed depending on whether the competitors were:

- racing alone against the clock,
- riding in a time trial with teammates who were setting the pace, or
- racing with teammates who were setting the pace plus competitors from other teams.

He found that the presence of pacemakers produced much faster times than when cycling alone, but that cycling with pacemakers and competitors produced the fastest times.

SOCIAL FACILITATION ▶ *improvement in performance when partnered or competing with others compared with performing solo.*

He considered the factors that might account for this result: perhaps the presence of other cyclists riding alongside the competitors might reduce wind resistance, thus increasing speeds, or perhaps team mates had been shouting encouragement and this had had a motivational effect. To test these hypotheses, he moved from the cycle track to the laboratory and constructed a piece of apparatus comprising fishing reels attached to a recording apparatus. Using children as participants, he asked them to wind in the fishing reels as fast as possible. The children worked alone or in pairs. He found that the mere presence of another child was enough to produce faster performance times. This was the first experimental demonstration of what became known as *social facilitation* (see Chapter 6).

A League of American Wheelmen cycle race, where Norman Triplett observed that providing both pacemakers and competitors resulted in the fastest times.

PROFESSIONAL PSYCHOLOGY

Psychology developed as an academic discipline, in part, as a means of addressing philosophical issues about the nature of what it is to be human in an empirical rather than speculative manner. For psychologists such as Wilhelm Wundt (1832–1920), the primary goal of psychology was pure research. However, the applied dimensions of psychology were never far away. The Galtonian roots of psychometric theory were intertwined, at least for the early years of its development, with eugenics, which was to be a practical guide to improving the human population by selective breeding. According to B.F. Skinner (1904–90), learning theory was, above all else, a technology for improving human life. The psychoanalytic movement began 'on the couch' in Sigmund Freud's (1856–1939) consulting room as he treated patients suffering from *hysteria* and *neuroses*. For Freud and his followers, psychoanalysis and associated psychotherapies were always a professional practice. Lightner Witmer (1867–1956) set up the first psychological clinic in 1896, treating children with learning problems, and describing himself as a clinical psychologist in 1907. In 1921, James McKeen Cattell (1860–1944), Robert S. Woodworth (1869–1962) and Edward Thorndike (1874–1949) set up the Psychological Corporation to sell psychological tests to government and industry. Hugo Münsterberg (1863–1916) wrote *On the Witness Stand: Essays on Psychology and Crime* (1908) and *Psychology and Industrial Efficiency* (1913), contributing to the development of forensic and industrial psychology. The regulation of these various strands of applied psychology began in the UK in the 1950s when, in 1954, the British Psychological Society (BPS) prepared the first draft of an ethical code on the standards of professional conduct for psychologists. The regulatory function of the BPS was handed over to the Health Professions Council (HPC) in 2009, which oversees professions including social workers and paramedics. In the USA, psychologists are licensed at the state or province level before being allowed to practise professionally.

James McKeen Cattell, along with Robert Woodworth and Edward Thorndike, set up the Psychological Corporation in 1921.

Experimental Replication Crisis – Faked
Research Data – Moral and Ethical Issues –
Positive Psychology – Cognitive Neuroscience
– Wearable Technologies –
Real-time Data Collection

FAKED
DATA

CHERRY-PICKING

CIA AND
ENHANCED
INTERROGATION

REPLICATION
CRISIS

ETHICS

CHALLENGES

RETRACTION
WATCH

POPULARITY

OPEN SCIENCE
COLLABORATION

FUTURE OF
PSYCHOLOGY

POSITIVE
PSYCHOLOGY

COGNITIVE
NEUROSCIENCE

WEARABLE
TECHNOLOGIES

COLLECTION OF
PRIVATE DATA

ECOLOGICAL
MOMENTARY
ASSESSMENT

THE POPULARITY OF PSYCHOLOGY

We've now looked at the major areas of psychology, so I hope you have some sense of psychology's great variety and diversity of theories and methods. Psychology as an academic discipline has grown remarkably over the last hundred or so years. From Wundt's Institute of Experimental Psychology, at the University of Leipzig, in 1879, initially staffed by Wundt and a few close colleagues, to today, a worldwide community of academic researchers and practitioners. In the UK, the British Psychological Society (BPS) has more than 60,000 members; in the USA, the American Psychological Association (APA) has over 150,000 members, who are all educated to doctorate (PhD) level. The International Psychoanalytical Association (IPA) has more than 11,500 members, drawn from 33 countries.

Worldwide community

Psychology is clearly a popular discipline that has a wide international scope. What then of the future prospects for the discipline? It is, of course, impossible to predict the future. But in this section I want to outline some of the current challenges psychology needs to face before going on to describe some potential future directions for research and theory.

CURRENT CHALLENGES

REPLICATION CRISIS ▶ *when the results of an important experiment cannot be repeated.*

Psychology's current challenges are methodological and ethical. The methodological challenges are related to what has become known as the ***replication crisis***. This is a crisis not of psychology in particular but of the sciences in general. One of the defining characteristics of scientific research is that scientists should be able to reproduce the results of their colleagues. By replicating the research and achieving the same results, other researchers can feel assured that the findings are robust and can be safely incorporated into other scientific studies. But since the beginning of the twenty-first century, more and more researchers have reported that when they attempt to repeat some of the most important experiments in fields including medicine, psychology, chemistry and biology they have not obtained the same significant results that were originally published in the scientific journals.

Replication crisis

THE OPEN SCIENCE COLLABORATION

Led by the American social psychologist Brian Nosek, the Open Science Collaboration, reported on attempts to replicate 100 psychology experiments. In the original experimental reports, 97 per cent of these studies found significant results; when repeated, this dropped to 36 per cent.

NAMES TO KNOW: HEALTH BELIEF MODEL

Brian Nosek (1974–present)

Martin Seligman (1942–present)

Michael Gazzaniga (1939–present)

George A. Miller (1920–2012)

This is very worrying. It means that psychological theories are being evaluated on the basis of faulty evidence, and time and money is being spent working on research projects that may well be a waste of time. Explanations for this failure to replicate include the pressure to publish significant results. It could well be the case that psychologists are sitting on data that does not support someone else's significant findings but that this data never gets published because journal editors prefer to publish dramatic and interesting results rather than papers that basically are reporting that there was no effect. This is related to researchers 'cherry picking' which studies they submit for publication and, through an act of self-censorship, not making their insignificant findings known. A number of proposals have been put forward to counter this problem. The first is for researchers to publicly share all raw data so that any interested researchers can go to the data and re-analyse it. A second proposal is that, to prevent 'cherry picking', researchers should pre-register their predictions before even collecting their data. In this way, it would become impossible to change one's hypotheses to fit the data and so keep researchers' experimental results 'honest'.

These problems of replication primarily stem from biases in how results are subsequently published. A more shocking problem has been the discovery that a number of researchers have simply faked their data. Diederik Stapel, professor of cognitive social psychology and dean of the School of Social and Behavioral Sciences at the University of Tillburg, was found to have used faked data that appeared in at least 30 published, peer-reviewed papers. This level of sustained deception is truly remarkable, but the pressures on researchers to obtain 'good results' in order to obtain research funding or academic progression are strong and some may be tempted into academic dishonesty.

Diederik Stapel, a professor of cognitive social psychology at the University of Tillburg, was at the centre of a scandal involving faked data.

RETRACTION WATCH

The organisation Retraction Watch tracks the notices published in academic journals that warn that research papers have been withdrawn, either because there is doubt about the veracity of the research or because serious errors in the methods or analysis have been discovered.

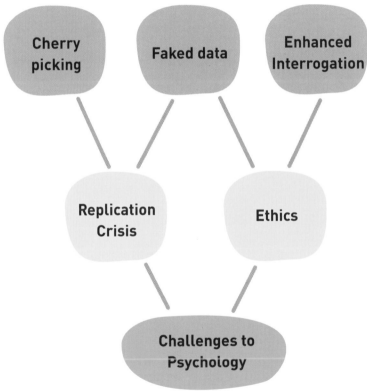

The final challenge is related to how psychological knowledge is used and the responsibilities of professional psychologists. In 2002, psychologists John Bruce Jessen and James Mitchell were contracted to work for the US Central Intelligence Agency (CIA) to advise on psychological approaches to interrogation. Working backwards from techniques designed to increase resistance to interrogation, they designed a programme of 'enhanced interrogation' that included waterboarding, sleep deprivation and being forced to adopt stress positions for long periods of time.

Psychologists have recently come under fire for their work in assisting the CIA, especially in regards to the development of 'enhanced. interrogation' techniques.

Newspaper reports state that their private company was paid up to $81 million for designing and administering this programme. As members of the American Psychological Association, they were bound to the ethical principle of 'do no harm'. Jessen and Mitchell defended the use of these techniques against accusations that they were torture on the grounds that they did **not** cause physical harm and, as psychologists, they were able to assess whether or not the person subjected to waterboarding was fit to continue the interrogation. Their very presence as psychologists ensured that waterboarding was not torture! The case raises important issues about the relationship between professional psychology and government.

Critics have argued that the APA tailored its ethical standards to the demands of the US administration and ignored the conflict of interest posed by those members who had held consulting roles with the Department of Defence or CIA. The journal *Nature* published an editorial in 2015 with the title *Lessons must be learned after psychology torture inquiry*, criticising the collusion between psychologists and security services to allow torture. One of the key challenges that lies ahead will be to maintain ethical standards in the face of increasing demands to loosen them on the grounds of national security or political expediency.

Current Trends

Over the last twenty years, the current trends in psychological research have been towards an increase in both professional and public interest in *positive psychology* and the neurosciences. *Positive psychology* Positive psychology takes as its starting point not the personal and social dilemmas and problems that have motivated much psychological research, but to focus very strongly on human strengths. The positive psychology movement is closely associated with the work of the social psychologist Martin Seligman (1942–present), who has written a series of popular self-help books aimed at popularising the approach. Examples of self-help exercises drawn from positive psychology include writing 'gratitude letters' that encourage writing a letter thanking someone for something they have done to help or support us and that we have never previously acknowledged.

POSITIVE PSYCHOLOGY ▶ *focuses on human strengths.*

Other techniques include ending each day by writing down three good things that happened that day and explaining why they happened. Seligman and his colleagues are developing a positive psychotherapy that aims not just to reduce negative symptoms but to but to build positive emotions and creativity. Pointing to traditional textbooks of clinical and abnormal psychology, they make the point that the content is devoted to accounts of feelings of shame, anxiety, guilt and depression and there is next to no discussion of curiosity, creativity, joy or love. The positive psychology movement is stimulating much current research and has some affinity with many of the techniques used by cognitive behavioural therapists and also the values of humanistic psychology (see Chapter 9).

It is likely to continue to develop, not least because the techniques it uses are open to everyone because they are inexpensive and 'low tech'. This is in sharp contrast to the other current trend in psychology, which is towards neuroscience and is decidedly 'high tech', led by the development of cheaper and cheaper brain imaging equipment. Cognitive neuroscience addresses the biological foundation of human cognition. The term was invented by two people. One was Michael Gazzaniga, a psychologist famous for his pioneering studies of the cognitive functions of individuals whose left and right brain hemispheres had been surgically separated after brain injury or to treat disease. The other was George A. Miller (first mentioned in Chapter 3), one of the founders of modern cognitive psychology.

Computational neuroscience uses mathematical models to understand how the brain works.

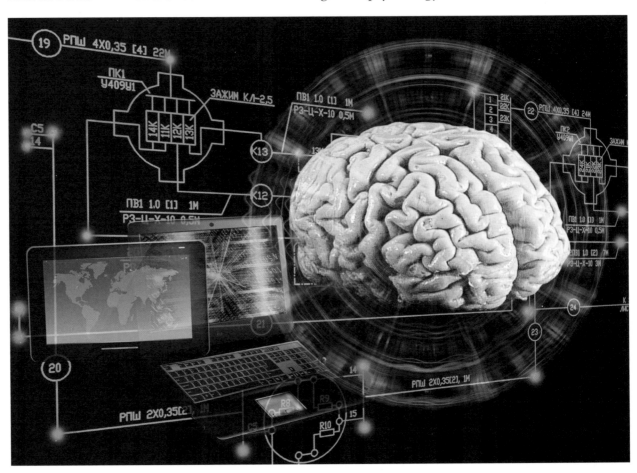

Gazzaniga and Miller conceived cognitive neuroscience as being at the interface between *systems neuroscience* (the study of neural pathways and circuits), *computational neuroscience* (the study of brain function by the development of mathematical models) and *cognitive psychology*. When Gazzaniga and Miller coined the term and defined the cognitive neuroscience research programme, computational neuroscience was still in its infancy and its models were rather simplistic. Systems neuroscience was, perhaps, even less well developed because, as we have seen, for many years EEG was the only available technology for measuring the firing of neural pathways. Cognitive psychology was the most highly developed of the three.

Systems and computational neuroscience

NEUROSCIENCE

COGNITIVE NEUROSCIENCE
the study of the biology behind human cognition

COMPUTATIONAL NEUROSCIENCE
the study of brain function by the development of mathematical models

SYSTEMS NEUROSCIENCE
the study of neural pathways and circuits

Brain imaging studies

Today, the methods of systems neuroscience and computational neuroscience have grown in sophistication and power and now, it might be argued, cognitive psychology is the junior partner. The technology of fMRI has become much cheaper for laboratories to purchase, leading to an explosion of imaging studies. Some of these **brain imaging studies** have been reported rather inaccurately in the press and in popular science books, leading to what has been referred to as 'neurobollocks', in which over-inflated claims about understanding what our brains 'really think' are passed over as scientific fact. The current popularity for brain imaging is likely to increase (see the next section) but it is unlikely that the role of psychology will decrease. Rather, the explosion of brain imaging studies have shown that the data they reveal can only be fully understood in conjunction with careful psychological research.

Wearable technologies like heart-rate monitors can provide a wealth of information for psychologists.

FUTURE DIRECTIONS

At the beginning of this chapter, I stated that predicting the future is impossible. However, here are some predictions about the future of psychological research, based on current trends and speculations about future technological advances.

The Influence of Wearable Technologies

Wearable EEG technology is also being developed. Though unlikely to yield results in the short term, it may eventually be possible to produce wearable fMRI scanners! The use of so called *ecological momentary assessment* and *short message service* (SMS) texts allows the psychologist to monitor an individual's behaviours and experiences in everyday life almost from moment to moment. Each of these methods is capable of generating useful data but the promise in the future is that data from these different sources of data can be used by psychologists, in collaboration with health professionals and other social scientist, to develop models that integrate the psychological, physiological and behavioural domains.

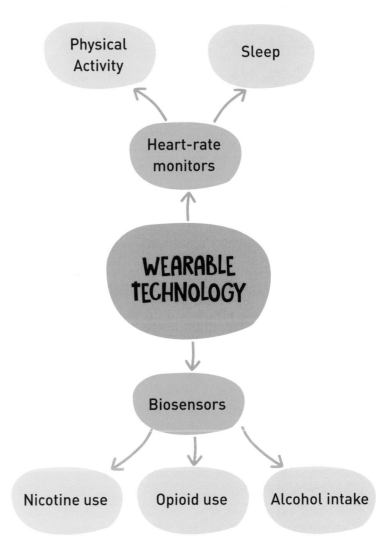

Continuous data collection

ECOLOGICAL MOMENTARY ASSESSMENT ▶ *studies individual behaviours in everyday life in real time.*

Given that these wearable sensors can be linked to mobile phone technology, the promise is that this data can be collected from thousands of participants and transmitted back to researchers who can monitor individuals and groups in real time and also analyse massive data sets comprising aggregated data. Mobile phone technology also includes geolocation data and it would be quite possible to map the movements and social interactions of users of this technology. Of course, with the collection of personal data there are also threats. These threats include invasion of privacy and concerns about how governments and business might use this data to control and manipulate citizens. We are entering a new and exciting era for psychology and psychologists but also one that will present challenges never faced, or even envisaged, before. Who knows where it may lead?

THE FACEBOOK SCANDAL

The use of Big Data in psychology is not without controversy. In 2017, Facebook was heavily criticised for allowing the psychologist Alexander Kogan to collect Big 5 personality data on 250,000 Facebook users, which was then sold on and used to tailor persuasive messages to particular personality profiles with the intention of maximising attitude change. Even more concerning, it appears that this data was obtained through misleading terms of service, and then was used by others to influence voters in the 2016 US presidential election. How effective targeting advertisements at individuals based on their personality profiles really is, at this time, not fully understood, but for academic psychologists, informed consent and participant confidentiality are fundamental ethical principles of professional practice. Such commercial and political motives are deeply problematic.

The Cambridge Analytica scandal has brought the threats of data collection home to the wider public – the future offers new possibilities for psychology, but there are many causes for concern as well.

GLOSSARY

1. *16PF*. A personality test designed by Raymond Cattell to measure the 16 factors he believed underlie differences in personality.

2. *ABC model of human behaviour.* A three-component model of attitudes comprising *Affect* (feeling), *Behaviour* (action) and *Cognition* (beliefs).

3. *Accommodation*. The term Piaget used to refer to the process by which a *Schema* (see below) is changed in response to new experiences.

4. *Assimilation*. The term Piaget used to refer to the process by which new experiences are 'edited' to fit into a pre-existing *Schema* (see below).

5. *Associationism*. A philosophical and psychological theory that knowledge, beliefs and actions are acquired through simple processes of pairing stimuli or responses with other stimuli.

6. *Attitude*. Readiness to respond to people, events and objects.

7. *Autonomic nervous system*. A part of the peripheral nervous system involved in involuntary and usually unconscious movement of organs including the heart and digestive system.

8. *Behaviourism*. A school of psychology that attempts to explain human behaviour in terms of external stimuli and responses. Behaviourist approaches to psychology are suspicious of mental constructs and attempt to explain human and animal actions in behavioural terms.

9. *Bivariate analysis*. The investigation of the relationship between two variables.

10. *Black box approach*. A model or theory that looks at the relationship between stimulus and response or input and output but does not investigate what intervenes between them.

11. *Brain waves* (*beta, alpha, theta and delta*). EEGs display the electrical activity of the brain in the form of brain waves. The frequency of these brainwaves is associated with different types of activity. They range from high-frequency *beta* waves, which occur when someone is solving a problem, to low-frequency *delta* waves, which occur during deep sleep.

12. *Cell theory of the brain*. The theory that psychological functions are associated with specific chambers (*ventricles*) of the brain. This theory dominated medical and psychological thinking from the ancient Greeks to the late seventeenth century.

13. *Cognitive behavioural therapy* (*CBT*). A form of treatment for a wide variety of psychological disorders that uses talk-based and behavioural techniques to control and eliminate unwanted feelings and thoughts.

14. *Cognitive dissonance*. Unpleasant feeling evoked when our actions and/or beliefs are inconsistent.

15. *Cognitive neuroscience*. The discipline that investigates the biological underpinnings of cognition.

16. *Computed tomography* (*computed axial tomography*) *scanning*. An imaging technique comprising multiple X-rays that are 'stitched together' using computer software to provide two- or three-dimensional representations of the brain.

17. *Conditioning* (*Pavlovian or classical*). A process of learning in which reflexes are paired with neutral stimuli (*unconditioned stimuli*) until the reflex response can be elicited by the presentation of the neutral stimulus alone (*conditioned response*). For example, blowing a puff of air through a straw into someone's eye and clicking ones fingers at the same time will, if repeated, eventually lead to that person blinking (*reflex response*) when the fingers are clicked and no air is blown into the eye.

18. *Conditioning* (*operant*) *behaviour.* Behaviour emitted by an organism that re-occurs if it leads to the reduction of a drive. For example, behaviour that leads to the presentation of food will continue until the organism is sated and has no further drive for food.

19. *Conditioned and unconditioned stimulus* – see *Conditioning* above.

20. *Contralateral function*. That the left hemisphere of the brain controls the right side of the body and vice versa.

21. *Decision model of bystander intervention*. An account of the steps and barriers that a person must undergo before choosing to help someone.

22. *Dementia praecox*. Literally, premature dementia. A term used by Emil Kraepelin to describe what we now refer to as schizophrenia.

23. *Dichotic listening*. A task in which a subject wearing headphones is presented with different auditory stimuli to the left ear from that presented to the right ear and instructed to listen or pay attention to both or only one of the sources.

24. *Dominant and non-dominant responses*. Dominant responses are well learned and practised actions requiring little thought. Non-dominant responses are unlearned and unpractised actions that need to be carefully monitored in order to be carried out correctly.

25. *Ego*. The term used by Freud to refer to that part of the mind that is governed by the reality principle and maps most closely to our conscious experience of ourselves.

26. *Electroencephalography* (*EEG*). A technique used to record electrical activity in the cortex of the brain via electrodes placed on the scalp.

27. *Enculturation*. The conscious or unconscious learning of cultural standards and symbols.

28. *Eysenck personality questionnaire* (*EPQ*). An instrument designed by Hans Eysenck to measure the personality traits of *extraversion*, *neuroticism* and *psychoticism*.

29. *Eugenics*. The term first used by Francis Galton to refer to a movement dedicated to improving the hereditary characteristics of human populations through selective breeding.

30. *Factor analysis*. Statistical technique that allows the observed correlations between a large number of variables to be re-described in terms of a smaller number of latent or unobserved 'factors' or dimensions that are thought to underlie the observed pattern.

31. *Filter theory of attention*. A theory proposed by Donald Broadbent to explain how the brain's limited information processing system avoids becoming overloaded by the sheer amount of information presented by the senses.

32. *Five factor theory*. A trait theory (*see below*) that explains individual differences in personality in terms of the following five dimensions (traits): openness to experience, conscientiousness, extraversion, agreeableness and neuroticism.

33. *Fluid and crystallised intelligence*. Fluid intelligence is the ability to solve novel problems using logic and abstract reasoning. Crystallised intelligence is the ability to use previously learned knowledge and experience that has been acquired over a life time.

34. *Forgetting curve*. Graph showing how much material is retained over time.

35. *General intelligence (g)*. A theory of the structure of intelligence proposed by Charles Spearman that there is a single factor that

underlies all intelligent activity, which he called 'g'.

36. *Genetic epistemology*. The term Piaget used to describe his developmental theory of knowledge.

37. *Gestalt*. A term used to refer to structures that cannot be understood by simply adding together their constituent parts. For example, the same four musical notes can be re-arranged to form very different melodies.

38. *Group think*. Irving Janis used the term to explain how decision making can be poor when made by groups who do not seek outside input or who do not listen to internal criticisms or alternative viewpoints.

39. *Health belief model*. A theory used extensively by health psychologists to understand and explain why people engage in health-related behaviours.

40. *Id*. The term Freud used to refer to that part of the mind that is governed by the pleasure principle. The *id* does not follow the rules of logic and its functioning is largely unconscious.

41. *Idiographic and nomothetic approaches*. Idiographic methods seek to understand a single person or event in all its individuality. Nomothetic methods seek to understand people or events by identifying what they have in common with other people or events.

42. *Implicit association*. Connections between different concepts that are elicited without the control of an individual.

43. *Intelligence quotient* (*IQ*). Originally calculated by dividing the mental age at which a child is performing by their chronological age and multiplying by 100 to give an indication of whether the child is functioning above or below average. It is now used to refer to the standardised scores on intelligence tests. The mean IQ is set at 100 with a standard deviation of 15 points.

44. *Introspection*. The examination or observation of one's own mental contents. Psychologists have argued intensively about whether introspection can be fitted into objective, scientific inquiry.

45. *Introversion and extraversion*. In personality theory, introversion and extraversion are the poles of a dimension that distinguishes those who are very outgoing and sociable from those who are withdrawn and internally focussed.

46. *Lexical approach*. A method of studying personality that starts from the hypothesis that all important ways of referring to individual differences are encoded into language.

47. *Likert scale*. Method of measuring attitudes usually using five- or seven-point scales.

48. *Neuroticism and stability*. In personality theory, neuroticism is one pole of a dimension that distinguishes people who are anxious, moody and fretful from those at the other pole (*stability*) who are calm and controlled.

49. *Phrenology*. Falsified nineteenth century attempt to localise brain function and understand personality by examining the bumps and hollows of the skull.

50. *Pneuma*. The ancient Greek belief that the living being was animated by the movement of air or breath (*pneuma*). They believed that cognition was brought about by the movement of *pneuma* through the ventricles of the brain (see *Cell theory of the brain* above).

51. *Psychiatry*. Medical speciality that studies and treats mental illness.

52. *Psychoanalysis*. Method of treating neuroses invented by Sigmund Freud that involved uncovering the unconscious through dream analysis.

53. *Psychometrics*. Approach to psychology that uses the methods of correlation and *factor analysis* to devise tests and models of intelligence and personality.

54. *Psychopathology*. The study of mental illness from a medical perspective.

55. *Psychophysics*. The systematic study of the relationship between physical stimuli and our sensations of those stimuli.

56. *Psychoticism*. In Eysenck's theory of personality, psychoticism is one pole of a dimension that distinguishes people who are reckless, hostile and impulsive from those at the other end of the dimension who can get on with others and accept social norms.

57. *Psychotherapy*. The use of psychological methods (talking therapies) rather than medical methods (drugs) to treat mental illness or distress.

58. *Realistic group conflict theory*. Muzafer Sherif's theory that competition for scarce resources results in bias, prejudice and aggressive behaviour.

59. *Rehearsal*. Repeated processing of material occupying the short-term memory that helps transfer the material to long-term memory.

60. *Reinforcement*. The application of a stimulus that increases the likelihood that a behaviour will be emitted (see *Operant conditioning* above).

61. *Scaffolding*. A term used by Bruner and developed from the work of Vygotsky to describe how a teacher can support student learning by providing help at the right time and then withdrawing that help when no longer needed.

62. *Schema*. A term used by Piaget and Bartlett to refer to the mental structures used to organise knowledge, beliefs and actions.

63. *Shaping*. The process by which complex behaviours are acquired through the precise use of *Reinforcement* (see *Operant conditioning* above).

64. *Short-term memory/long-term memory*. In multi-store theories of memory, short-term memory has a limited capacity (7 + or – 2 bits of information). Long-term memory has unlimited capacity. Items can

transfer from short-term memory to long-term memory by means of *Rehearsal* (see above).

65. *Social facilitation*. Increased productivity when in the presence of an audience.

66. *Social identity theory*. The theory that the mere categorisation of people into groups is enough to produce bias and prejudice. (Contrast with *Realistic group conflict theory* above).

67. *Stage theories*. Accounts of human development that posit distinct phases rather than gradual change.

68. *Traits*. In psychometric theories of personality, traits are relatively enduring dispositions to respond. *Factor analysis* (see above) is used to identify how many traits underlie human personality. Psychologists have arrived at different models including Eysenck's three-trait model, the *Five factor* (*trait*) *model* and Cattell's *16 trait model*.

69. *Transcranial magnetic stimulation*. A non-invasive method using magnetic fields to stimulate brain activity.

70. *Völkerpsychologie*. The term used by Wilhelm Wundt to describe historical and comparative approaches to the study of shared cultural beliefs and norms.

71. *Working memory model*. The theory of how information is stored and manipulated during problem solving.

72. *Zone of proximal development*. The term introduced by Vygotsky to refer to the problem-solving capacities of a child requiring the support of a teacher. These capacities eventually become fully internalised and the presence of the teacher is no longer necessary. The child can then tackle more difficult problems requiring more complex capacities that again will need teacher support at first before becoming internalised.

SUGGESTED READING

1. WHAT IS PSYCHOLOGY?
General Reading
Slater, L. (2005). *Opening Skinner's Box: Great Psychological Experiments of the 20th Century*. London: Bloomsbury. Good descriptions of classic psychology experiments.
Richards, G. (2010). *Putting Psychology in its Place: Critical Historical Perspectives* (3rd ed.). London: Routledge. A textbook that puts the history of psychology into its social context.
Websites
The British Psychological Society website provides careers advice on becoming a psychologist and general information on the scope of the profession.
https://www.bps.org.uk
The British Psychological Society Research Digest showcases psychological research.
https://digest.bps.org.uk/
Classics in the History of Psychology is an electronic resource that hosts original papers written by the founders of modern psychology. Papers by many of the authors mentioned in the book (from Wundt to Bandura) can be read and downloaded free of charge from this website.
http://psychclassics.yorku.ca/

2. PSYCHOLOGY OF LEARNING
Rutherford, A. (2009). *Beyond the Box: B.F. Skinner's Technology of Behavior from Laboratory to Life, 1950s–1970s*. Toronto: University of Toronto Press. Puts Skinner's work in to social context.
Toates, F. M. (2009). *Burrhus F. Skinner: the Shaping of Behaviour*. Basingstoke: Palgrave Macmillan. Good technical account of Skinner's approach to learning.
Todes, D. P. (2014). *Ivan Pavlov: A Russian Life in Science*. Oxford: Oxford University Press. In depth biography of Pavlov.

3. BIOLOGICAL PSYCHOLOGY
Sacks, O. (2011). *The Man Who Mistook His Wife for a Hat*. London: Picador. The famous neurologist describes the case histories of patients suffering from a wide variety of cognitive defecits.
Zimmer, C. (2005). *Soul Made Flesh: The Discovery of the Brain – and How it Changed the World*. New York: Free Press. Non-technical account of the development of the brain sciences.

4. PSYCHOLOGY OF COGNITION
Eysenck, M. W. & Keane, M. T. (2015). *Cognitive Psychology: A Student's Handbook* (7th ed.). London; New York: Psychology Press, Taylor & Francis Group. Comprehensive general textbook.
Miller, G. A. (1991). *Psychology: The Science of Mental Life* (Reprinted). New York, NY: Penguin Books. Classic statement of the then new cognitive psychology.
Baddeley, A. D. (1999). *Essentials of Human Memory*. Hove, England: Psychology Press. Thorough and expert account of the memory literature.

5. DEVELOPMENTAL PSYCHOLOGY
Keenan, T., Evans, S., & Crowley, K. (2016). *An Introduction to Child Development* (3rd ed.). Los Angeles: SAGE. Good general textbook.
Gopnik, A., Meltzoff, A. N., & Kuhl, P. K. (2001). *How Babies Think: the Science of Childhood*. London: Phoenix. Textbook written by active researchers that provides an excellent introduction to developmental psychology.
Piaget, J. (2001). *The Psychology of Intelligence*. London; New York: Routledge. Classic account of the development of intelligence by one of the foremost psychologists of the twentieth century.
Vygotsky, L. S., & Kozulin, A. (1986). *Thought and Language* (Translation newly rev. and edited). Cambridge, Mass: MIT Press. Book that brought the work of Vygotsky to the attention of western developmental psychologists.

6. SOCIAL PSYCHOLOGY
Blass, T. (2009). *The Man Who Shocked the World: the Life and Legacy of Stanley Milgram*. New York: Basic Books. Account of the life and times of one of the most influential twentieth century social psychologists.
Hogg, M. A. & Vaughan, G. M. (2013). *Social Psychology* (7th ed.). Harlow: Pearson Education. Well regarded general text book.
Smith, J. R., & Haslam, S. A. (Eds.). (2017). *Social Psychology: Revisiting the Classic Studies* (2nd ed.). Los Angeles: SAGE. The most important experiments in social psychology clearly described and critically evaluated.
Fox, D., Prilleltensky, I., & Austin, S. (Eds). (2009). *Critical Psychology: An Introduction* (2nd ed.). Los Angeles; London: SAGE. Classis statement of critical psychology.
Gergen, K. J. (2001). *Social Construction in Context*. London; Thousand Oaks, Calif: SAGE. One of social psychology's elder statesmen offers a new approach to researching the subject.

7. CLINICAL PSYCHOLOGY
Bentall, R. P. (2009). *Doctoring the Mind: Is Our Current Treatment of Mental Illness Really Any Good?* New York: New York University Press. Provocative account of the drug treatment of mental illness by a distinguished clinical psychologist.
Byron, T. (2015). *The Skeleton*

Cupboard: Stories of Sanity, Madness and Hope. A clinical psychologist describes the ups and downs of clinical practice.
Llewelyn, S. P. & Murphy, D. J. (Eds). (2014). *What is Clinical Psychology?* (5th ed.). Oxford: Oxford University Press. Guide for students wishing to pursue a career in clinical psychology.
Davey, G. (2014). *Psychopathology: Research, Assessment and Treatment in Clinical Psychology* (2nd ed.). [UK]: Chichester, West Sussex: The British Psychological Society; Wiley. Good general text book.
Ward, I. & Zarate, O. (2007). *Introducing Psychoanalysis: A Graphic Guide*. London: Icon Books Ltd Freud explained in cartoons without dumbing down difficult concepts.

8. PSYCHOLOGY OF PERSONALITY
Corr, P. J. (2016). *Hans Eysenck*. London; New York, NY: Palgrave Macmillan. Account of the career of one of the UK's most famous psychologists.
Chamorro-Premuzic, T. (2011). *Personality and Individual Differences* (2nd ed.). Hoboken, NJ: BPS Blackwell. Good general text book.
Maltby, J., Day, L., & Macaskill, A. (2013). *Personality, Individual Differences and Intelligence*. Text book

that covers intelligence and personality in one volume.

9. PSYCHOLOGY OF INTELLIGENCE
Gould, S. J. (1996). *The Mismeasure of Man* (Rev. and expanded). New York: Norton. Controversial critique of the psychometric approach to IQ testing.
Mackintosh, N. J. (2011). *IQ and Human Intelligence* (2nd ed.). Oxford; New York: Oxford University Press. Thorough account of research on human intelligence.
Kline, P. (2000). *A Psychometrics Primer*. London: Free Association. Short guide explaining in non-technical terms the technique of factor analysis.

10. PROFESSIONAL PSYCHOLOGY
Crighton, D. A., Towl, G. J. & British Psychological Society (Eds). (2015). *Forensic Psychology* (2nd ed.). Chichester, West Sussex, UK; Malden, MA: John Wiley & Sons Inc. Good general text.
Ogden, J. (2012). *Health Psychology: a textbook* (5th ed.). Maidenhead: Open University Press. Good general text.
Tod, D., Thatcher, J., & Rahman, R. (2010). *Sport Psychology*. New York: Palgrave Macmillan. Good general text.

Lewis, R., & Zibarras, L. (Eds). (2013). *Work and Occupational Psychology: Integrating Theory and Practice*. London: SAGE. Good general text.

11. FUTURE DIRECTIONS
Seligman, M. E. P. (2011). *Flourish: A New Understanding of Happiness and Well-being, and How to Achieve Them*. London: Brealey. Self-help book from one of the founders of positive psychology.
'Outside Psychologists Shielded U.S. Torture Program, Report Finds' - *The New York Times*. (n.d.). Retrieved May 29, 2018, from **https://www.nytimes.com/2015/07/11/us/psychologists-shielded-us-torture-program-report-finds.html**, newspaper article describing the collusion of psychologists with the military to carry out torture.
Bagot, K. S., Matthews, S. A., Mason, M., Squeglia, L. M., Fowler, J., Gray, K., Patrick, K. (2018). 'Current, future and potential use of mobile and wearable technologies and social media data in the ABCD study to increase understanding of contributors to child health.' *Developmental Cognitive Neuroscience*. **https://doi.org/10.1016/j.dcn.2018.03.008** New article that introduces the new wearable technologies and explains

how they might be used to study child neuropsychological development.
Gibney, E. (2018, March 29). 'The scant science behind Cambridge Analytica's controversial marketing techniques [News].' **https://doi.org/10.1038/d41586-018-03880-4**, article in the journal *Nature*, which suggests that the scientific underpinning of the Cambridge Analytica story may be rather weak.

INDEX